THE BUTTERFLY FRIENDLY GARDEN

For Marcus and Trudy

THE BUTTERFLY FRIENDLY GARDEN

Make your garden the perfect place for butterflies

Andrew George

a&i

Alphabet and Image Publishers
77 High Street
Totnes
Devon TQ9 5PB

Published by Alphabet and Image Publishers 2007

ISBN 978-1-899296-32-3

A CIP catalogue record for this book is available from the British Library.

The publishers and the author disclaim any injury, damage, loss or liability connected
with the use of the activities in this book. There may be unintentional errors or
omissions. In this case, please contact the publishers.

Printed and bound in China on paper supplied from a managed resource.

Contents

Foreword

by Alan Titchmarsh MBE VMH

Vice President of Butterfly Conservation

To me, a garden without butterflies is a lifeless place, but drop in a brimstone, a few small tortoiseshells and a red admiral or two and excitement and wonder are guaranteed. It's inspiring to be able to find out how we can create butterfly habitats in our own gardens. These 'flying flowers' might be less common nowadays but they will often appear unexpectedly in their wandering journeys across the countryside. Although flower-rich meadows, light woodland and hedgerows are the usual places where butterflies and moths can live and breed, and where we can observe and enjoy them, gardens are becoming part of that network. If we make conscious efforts to include nectar-rich plants for the adults and larval foodplants for caterpillars to feed on, then these special creatures will become frequent visitors and may even set up colonies in our own back yards.

The Butterfly Friendly Garden describes a range of outdoor areas – from patios to borders, in gardens large and small – that can be designed with butterflies in mind. There are specific plants, useful to a wide range of species, which will attract the various butterfly families. Sun, shelter, even how the ground is shaped, can turn an ordinary garden into a butterfly haven.

The result will be a colourful oasis that welcomes wild creatures and helps to link up the patchwork of areas where they can find refuge. So take up the challenge now. It doesn't take much in the way of effort to enable you to play your part in preserving native wildlife in your own butterfly friendly garden.

Introduction

Small gardens, large gardens, front gardens, back yards, paths, driveways and even roofs can all be shaped and planted to attract butterflies. It is something that many of us could do to help the environment in a direct way. We can all get our hands dirty making a

butterfly garden or meadow – a nature reserve that really counts. Butterflies like warmth, shelter and an abundance of plants rich in nectar. Even the smallest garden in a city centre can be made attractive to them by putting the right plants in the right places, and larger gardens may have the space for habitats that will encourage more unusual species. As the wider countryside becomes tidier, with hedges and fields cut, fertilised and sprayed, refuges for butterflies are becoming scarcer. Some species can travel large distances, but others are sedentary and will not fly over a hedge – never mind vast green fields rich in fertiliser and empty of flowers.

But it is possible to squeeze a lot into a little. To combat intensive farming methods, urban gardens can become intensive nature reserves and play an important part in providing food and shelter for butterflies as they move from place to place. And a garden that is rich in butterflies will also provide shelter for more secretive kinds of wild creature.

The Butterfly Friendly Garden features the butterflies that are most likely to be attracted to the projects I describe; there are British butterflies that are unlikely to visit a garden or plot of land because of their distribution, rarity or habitat requirements. I have concentrated on gardens and plants to attract British butterflies, but all the species and plants are found in other parts of northern Europe. Many of the projects should succeed in temperate gardens all over the world.

The book starts with the butterflies that are most often seen in gardens, showing how, using a mixture of native and garden plants, it is possible to attract them to a plot all year round, and not only during the month in which the buddleia is flowering.

The next two sections focus on natural habitats, describing how to create similar areas in the garden to attract species of butterfly more normally seen in the countryside. These species may be encouraged to stay and breed, or even set up permanent colonies. Whether you choose hay meadow, chalk downland, tussocky grass, scrub, hedgerow, woodland, wetland or pond, it is possible to include all these different types of habitat in a relatively small garden and still leave room for the barbecue. Creating different habitats also allows us to grow many of the most colourful and interesting of British wildflowers, a fascinating enterprise in itself.

The final section describes some of the best methods of propagating the most relevant wildflowers, while explaining how a small garden reserve can become part of a bigger environment. Counting butterflies and moths in an individual garden helps environmentalists assess how these species are faring in the wider world – some are currently expanding their range northwards as a response to global warming, others are confined to ever-smaller areas of land. By monitoring butterflies in your own garden you can add to naturalists' knowledge: spotting a new species visiting, or even staying in, your garden can bring a real sense of achievement.

Throughout the book there are references to foodplants and nectar plants. The foodplant is the plant which the butterfly's larvae feed on; the nectar plant is the one that butterflies use regularly as a nectar source.

If there are meadows or areas of wasteland near you, they will be home to a number of butterflies and moths. Knowing which species are present, and which plants attract them in these habitats, can help you to design your garden.

The reference books I recommend on page 189 contain distribution maps to help identify the butterflies of your area. Local experts can be found through the county branches of Butterfly Conservation.

My own interest in butterflies blossomed at the same time as my first wildflower meadow. After many false starts, I eventually created a meadow that I was pleased with. Butterflies began to arrive and I was hooked. Collaborating with Clive Farrell of Ryewater Nurseries in Dorset, I have been involved in designing many and varied habitats ever since.

Part One:
Garden Butterflies

Chapter One

Here Comes the Sun

Imagine an aerial view of a town or city. Near the centre a few green patches can be seen and, further out, larger blocks of park and wasteland but, most of all, there are gardens. From the air these resemble woodland, sandwiched between houses, with a scattering of open clearings made up of small lawns and flowerbeds, ponds and patios. Many natural habitats of the countryside also exist in towns, and even though many of the plants may have been introduced from other countries, this garden woodland is now frequently richer in wildlife than the fields beyond.

The butterflies we find in our own gardens are creatures of the sun. Their bodies need to

Male and female Green-veined White butterflies mating. The green veins are especially pronounced in the spring brood.

A Green-veined White basking in the morning sun. This is one of the most widespread butterflies and is commonly seen in gardens.

The Green-veined White

In flight, the Green-veined White looks very similar to the Small White, but at rest the pattern of darker scales that follows the veins on the underside of the wings is clearly visible.

The first Green-veined Whites emerge in early April, having over-wintered as chrysalises. These butterflies enjoy many of the habitats found in gardens but are especially attracted to warm, moist, lush vegetation. There are usually two broods a year, although in very warm years they may have a third. The broods almost overlap, as the last of the first brood can be flying when the first of the second appears.

Males emerge a few days earlier than the females and have a rather different agenda. Besides nectaring, a male's main activity will be the search for newly-emerged females: he will chase anything fluttery and white to check whether it is a female or a rival male. Often the object of his attentions will turn out to be a butterfly of another closely-related species, perhaps a Small White or an Orange-tip.

After mating the female searches for plants on which to lay her eggs. Although looking similar to both the Large and Small Whites (cabbage whites) she does not, like them, choose cabbages or other garden brassicas. Her search is for the seedlings, or small plants, of wild crucifers, and particularly garlic mustard, usually found in a humid, semi-shady spot, or lady's smock, which will thrive beside a pond.

Most butterflies are only really active when the sun is shining, although they will fly on warm overcast days. In the morning the adult butterfly will orientate its wings towards the sun, using them like solar panels, until its body reaches the right temperature for activity to take place. On hot days, butterflies regulate their body temperature by closing their wings to lose heat.

GARDEN BUTTERFLIES

warm up before they can fly, and they will use the open sunny areas to flit from garden to garden in search of nectar, mates, or plants to lay their eggs on – their foodplants.

The Spiral Garden at Ryewater Nursery, designed by Ivan Hicks, represents a butterfly's proboscis. A spiral path leads to a pond at the centre. The plants have mostly been selected for their attractiveness to butterflies and there are a number of open, sunny situations. A variety of habitats include the gravel path, 'tame-flower' meadow, prairie, wetland, semi-shady spaces, woodland with understorey, and hedgerow.

THE FLOWER BORDER

With hedges and clearings, ponds, fences and paths, most gardens are full of edges. It is at these edges – the transition between one habitat and another – that much wildlife thrives, though in our gardens these boundaries are often quite sharply defined compared to those found in natural surroundings.

Out in the countryside, one of the favourite habitats of many butterflies is the region where a meadow rich in wildflowers flows into a south-facing hedge. Here it is sheltered and warm and a profusion of grasses and wildflowers provides nectar and foodplants. A flower

border backed by a hedge can act as a tempting substitute, and there are many things that can be done to make it more like the wild meadow, even using cultivated plants.

Gardeners have always made use of nectar-rich plants to attract butterflies. Favourites include aubretia and aster, candytuft and catmint, golden rod and hebe, ice plant (*Sedum spectabile*) and lavender, marigold and Michaelmas daisy, not to mention nasturtium and phlox, scabious and sweet William, verbena and wallflower. With an existing flower border a gradual transition can take place as more and more of these butterfly-friendly plants are added.

One of the first steps for a butterfly gardener is to learn to become more relaxed about what is visiting the garden. If you want to create a wildlife garden, then worry less about the traditional baddies: there are no insect enemies. If aphids invade, just wait until the hoverflies get them. In the initial stages of the garden there may be some weed problems, but gradually the border will reach equilibrium.

The Red Admiral unfurls its proboscis to nectar on a wallflower. The proboscis is like a straw that the sugar-rich nectar is sucked through. This solution of sugars fuels its hectic life.

A TAMEFLOWER MEADOW

A flower border or larger area of ground can be converted into what I call a 'tameflower' meadow, by stocking it with perennials and grasses that may have come originally from all over the world. The inclusion of grasses will give the border a more natural appearance, and the development of continuous cover plus minimal disturbance to the soil will encourage various forms of wildlife.

A wild meadow has large numbers of perennial plants from a few key genera – buttercup and sorrel, ox-eye daisy and knapweed. The tameflower meadow looks best with the same kind of continuity: a limited range of plants, but growing in profusion. Many asters, knapweeds and scabious are good sources of nectar. Here and there, interesting individual plants can be planted amongst the swathes of the few, to act as focal points to draw the eye.

Many grasses blend happily into a tameflower meadow, but there are five in particular which provide a range of sizes, and form a good background for the flowers. *Briza media* subspecies *elatior* is a larger version of quaking grass and shimmers in the sun. *Festuca amethystina* is a fine fescue and has a purple haze of flowering heads. *Sporoborus heterolepis* is a North

Asters and Trifolium rubens *dominate this part of the tameflower meadow*

American prairie grass and creates a hemisphere of copper seed heads in the autumn. *Chionochloa rubra* forms a large clump of fine, long, arching grasses and, almost two metres high, *Stipa gigantea* has seed heads of shimmering gold.

Not too long after introducing grasses to your border you will find that the flowers and grasses together have begun to form a continuous ground cover and the main task will be to weed out anything you do not want. By autumn the grasses will be a golden tapestry of waving seed heads.

There is a long list of individual species to grow among the grasses. The butterfly gardener is always searching for the best provider of nectar, and one good candidate is *Verbena bonariensis* – a plant to rival buddleia. Focal points in a large meadow could also include the tall yellow scabious, *Cephalaria gigantea*, and a globe thistle, *Echinops exaltatus*. Both are also good nectar plants.

In autumn the grasses are the stars of the show. Supporting the act is Verbena bonariensis.

Around the house

Butterflies are as highly visible as birds, though it's possible to approach them much more closely. And, like birds, they can be watched from a window. Butterfly enthusiast, Lyn Formison, has not only surrounded her house with butterfly-friendly plants but has pots of buddleia, pruned in succession to flower at different times, which can be moved close to the windows.

Buddleia 'Lochinch', which is a cross between *Buddleia davidii* and *Buddleia fallowiana* and an excellent nectar plant, surrounds the back door. Outside the kitchen window Lyn has used the perennial wallflower, 'Bowles Mauve', and Corsican crosswort, *Phuopsis stylosa*. Cutting this back after it has flowered will result in a second flowering. She has also planted *Clematis heracleifolia* 'Wyevale' to attract Red Admirals, and marjoram, teasel, lavender, ice plant and honesty are all visible as she stands at the sink.

Butterfly-friendly plants close to the windows of Lyn Formison's home in Hampshire.

Starting from scratch

To create a flower border or tameflower meadow from scratch, one of the simplest methods is to mark out the area for the border in a sunny, sheltered spot and then lay down biodegradable eco-matting. All the unwanted weed seeds and perennial roots will be trapped under the mat and soon die from lack of light.

The mat should be covered with a thin layer of weed-free soil – nutrient-poor material is probably the best. Then the selected butterfly plants can be planted through slits cut in the mat, where they will flourish in the absence of competition.

Within four or five years the mat will start to deteriorate, but by then the cycle of annual weeds will have been broken. One of the main problems initially is distinguishing the seedlings of the grasses you want to keep from those you want to weed out; experience will soon teach you the difference.

Wildflowers for nectar

Among the best sources of nectar are our own native wildflowers. Some of these plants will find their own way in, but others can be introduced and will fit very well among garden plants.

There are advantages to growing wildflowers in a garden context. They are frequently tougher than nursery-bought garden plants and seem not to be so affected by the usual pests and diseases. Some of them are just as showy, indeed, many of the best nectar plants are also the most colourful. They need not be expensive; plugs can be bought in bulk from specialist nurseries quite cheaply, and a packet of wildflower seeds may contain hundreds, or even thousands, of potential plants.

Wildflowers that can be used to good effect in a border include Devil's-bit scabious, small scabious, field scabious, purple loosestrife, marjoram, betony, greater knapweed, valerian, viper's bugloss and tansy. Horseshoe vetch works particularly well in a rockery and can be the best nectar plant available at the time that it flowers, from mid-May to mid-June. The meadow thistle is an uncommon native, which grows to new heights in a garden. Other wildflowers may not be notable as sources of nectar, but have visual importance – greater burnet, dark mullein, dropwort, dyer's greenweed, meadow cranesbill, musk mallow, nettle-leaved bell-flower, orpine, saw-wort, small teasel, spiny restharrow, sweet cicely, water avens and woolly thistle, will all thrive and look well among traditional garden plants.

Peacock nectaring on Devil's-bit scabious, one of the best nectar plants.

The pond at Carymoor, Castle Cary, Somerset (see page 131). Marshy ground around the pond is an intense colour experience, with White butterflies and purple loosestrife, Orange-tips and pink ragged robin, Small Coppers and orange-gold fleabane, against a background of dark green reeds and rushes.

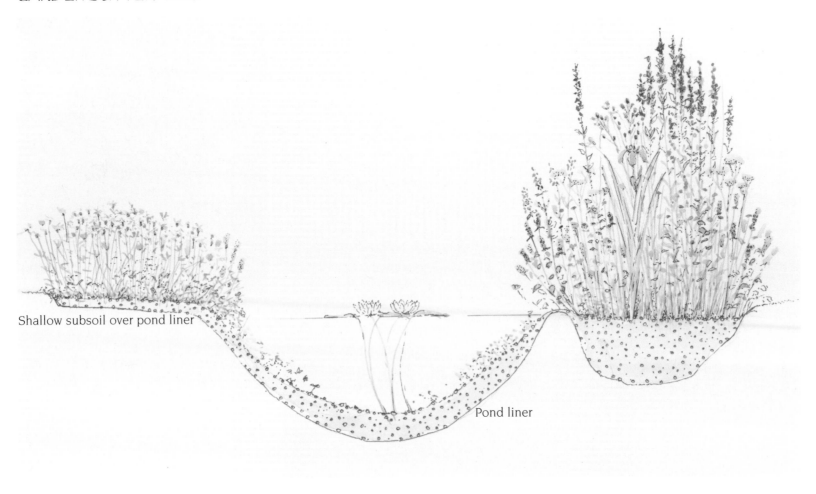

Shallow subsoil over pond liner

Pond liner

Extending the pond area to create a bog area.

PONDS AND BOG AREAS

Shady pools attract few butterflies, so to get the best out of a garden pond it should be sited out in the open. Here dragonflies will hawk over the surface and butterflies nectar on the margins.

Marshy ground next to a pond can be developed in one of two ways. Where a pond has been created using a liner or, much more cheaply, a couple of layers of damp-proof liner, another hole can be dug next to the pond and lined with similar material. This lining should be pierced in a few places to allow for some drainage, then the hole filled first with the excavated soil-rich topsoil, followed by the poorer subsoil. Once it is topped up with water the new bog area is ready to plant and seed.

The other way to create a wet area is to extend the pond liner beyond the pond (see diagram, above) and cover the extension with a layer of subsoil to a depth of a few centimetres. The soil keeps moist through osmosis and its low fertility makes it ideal for some of the lower-growing wetland plants, such as lady's smock. Ragged robin also loves a boggy situation. Like many other wildflowers, this is a plant that grows easily from seed and, sown into damp, bare, weed-free soil, will come up like cress. Purple loosestrife is a tall, dramatic wetland plant and one of the best sources of nectar, especially for White butterflies, if grown in a semi-shady situation. Speckled Woods will also nectar on it. Water mint, Devil's-bit scabious, fleabane and marsh woundwort are other nectar plants that thrive in marshy ground.

The Orange-tip

A close relative of the Green-veined White, the Orange-tip regularly comes into gardens. The male has orange tips to his forewings. The female looks similar to other small Whites when flying, but at rest you can see a beautiful mottled green pattern on the underside of the wings. Its behaviour is very similar to the Green-veined White, but the female is more likely to lay her eggs in open situations.

The Orange-tip has a similar range of foodplants as the Green-veined, but perhaps the favourite is lady's smock. Phlox and honesty, are also visited, although there have been reports that the caterpillars do not flourish on these. An unusual, striking wildflower that this butterfly does thrive on is the tower mustard (*Arabis glabra*).

ABOVE: *Male Orange-tip.*
LEFT: *Where lady's smock grows, it grows profusely, but in some gardens, the conditions are not right for it. Although you can buy plants, it is difficult to find a supplier of the seed. If you have trouble growing it, try tower mustard (see next page).*

ABOVE *Tower mustard grows easily from seed, but needs to be sown each year as it is a biennial. Collect the seed and sow in pots, to ensure you do not lose the plant from your garden.*
RIGHT *Orange-tip caterpillar on tower mustard. Young Orange-tip caterpillars start at the bottom of the tower, and slowly climb to the top. By the time they reach the 'penthouse' they are fully grown.*

Tower mustard

Tower mustard is a rare biennial found in only a few dry bare places, but it is easy to grow from seed and will settle quite happily into a border or rockery. If seed is not available, the plant can be found in specialist nurseries (see page 176).

Tower mustard starts as a rosette, almost like a small hawkbit. The next leaves are upright, then the flower spike appears and small creamy flowers burst open. The stalk continues to grow, with more flowers opening, until the plant is almost shoulder high. The seed heads develop, each pointing skyward. The plant now really is a tower but, long before such height is reached, the Orange-tip female has laid her eggs on the underside of the first flowers.

After a week the caterpillars hatch. At first they are tiny but as they feed on the seedpods they slowly make their way up the tower. Young Orange-tip caterpillars are cannibals and will eat any others that cross their path. By late June, there will be a few fat green caterpillars sitting on the tops of a large proportion of the towers. Most caterpillars are found on plants growing within a few metres of hedgerows, since they will eventually leave the plant to find tall vegetation in which to pupate.

ABOVE *Orange-tip pupa with the orange tips showing through.*
LEFT *Newly-emerged Orange-tip female.*

RAISED BEDS

Raised beds can be the answer to more than one gardening problem. They certainly reduce the need for bending when weeding. And sometimes nursery-bought plants fail to thrive when put out into cold wet garden soils; in a contained raised bed, soil can be specially mixed to provide a more favourable medium.

Railway sleepers are ideal as a frame; the 'container' they make should then be filled with a mixture of 80% grit and 20% stone and loam. This provides sharp drainage during the winter months but also conserves moisture around the individual particles, resulting in a soil that is well drained but moist. Many of the attractive Mediterranean plants loved by butterflies, as well as a range of other insects, can be grown very successfully in this type of soil.

One rare and interesting plant that thrives in a raised bed is tuberous thistle (*Cirsium tuberosum*). This dramatic addition to a flowerbed will prove a great attraction to butterflies, as will *Centranthus lecoqii*, a restrained relative of red valerian.

Grown in raised beds, Centranthus lecoqii (syn. C. ruber 'Mauve Form') *thrives at Phoenix Perennial Plants, Marina Christopher's specialist plant nursery in Hampshire. Most of her plants have been chosen for their benefit to insects. Towering above is the rare tuberous thistle.*

Telekia speciosa. Its golden daisy-like flowers make this one of the most popular butterfly nectar plants at Phoenix Perennial Plants. By looking out for butterflies at nurseries, you may spot unexpected sources of nectar.

THE THIRSTY LANDS

Whether for practical reasons of parking or ease of maintenance, areas of hard stone pavement and gravel now dominate many gardens, but this does not mean that they are lost to butterflies. Many species love to bask in the warmth of these sun-baked places and can then be persuaded to visit by strategically-placed containers of tempting nectar or food plants.

In a modern setting, tall sculptural thistles are very effective. Some thistles are both good sources of nectar for butterflies and the foodplants for Painted Ladies. Smaller nectar plants can be placed around the base of a thistle. All kinds of pots, troughs and basins can be used to grow a wide range of plants.

At Ryewater, Ivan Hicks has designed a prison for 'naughty' plants, prickly and stinging plants, such as thistles, nettles and brambles. Many of them are butterfly foodplants. Painted Ladies lay their eggs on the thistles and Small Tortoiseshells use the nettles. The whole area is also planted with thousands of thymes. The black and white gravel floor is enjoyed by butterflies basking in the sun.

ABOVE A *red form of kidney vetch in a stone trough.*
RIGHT Red *valerian thrives in challenging situations.*
BELOW RIGHT A *classical Georgian garden with nectar plants.*

In a more traditional setting, one of the best nectar plants for a hot, dry environment is red valerian. In the wild it can be found in the most inhospitable places, including the top of walls, abandoned quarries and cliff faces.

Creating a gravel garden

A low-maintenance gravel garden can be created if the gravel is kept separate from the underlying soil. A layer of geotextile matting, covered by a good 15cm (6in) of gravel, is all that is needed. Small particles of soil, twigs and moss will be washed down to lie on the matting and plants that like this sort of environment will send their roots down to this level and cling to it. Thrifts, eryngiums, echiums and thymes all do well in this situation.

At the seaside

A seaside garden will support a variety of plants accustomed to dry conditions. It can be made by covering a mound with geotextile matting, topped by a layer of sand.

An interesting planting arrangement in this situation would be lady's bedstraw, grown with viper's bugloss and red valerian, to create a yellow, blue and red combination. The plants will bake in the sand and Hummingbird Hawkmoths may be attracted to nectar on the valerian and bugloss. These large insects bear a strong resemblance to their namesake, with whirring wings and a long proboscis to probe for nectar. A female Hawkmoth will detect

Thrift revelling in gravel.

This sandy garden was created on a mound and is planted with seaside plants, including sea holly, horseshoe vetch, sea cabbage, viper's bugloss and lady's bedstraw.
BELOW Hummingbird Hawkmoth caterpillars feasting on lady's bedstraw.

the bedstraw while she is nectaring, and may lay a few eggs, which will hatch into a clutch of large green caterpillars.

Creating an exotic cornfield

In recent years there has been a vogue for sowing cornfield annuals to replicate the poppy-filled cornfields of the past. Wheat can be added to the poppies, cornflowers and corn marigolds to give the display a more authentic feel. This can be done on a small scale in the garden (see page 102), but an annual meadow can also be sown with more exotic plants, to make an interesting variation on the theme.

Perhaps the best site for an exotic annual cornfield, especially for tiny gardens or patios, would be a raised bed near the house. Using a raised bed or container would help keep weed seeds out, and provide a wonderful patch of colour during the summer.

The exotic annual meadow will need a grass, and *Briza maxima* fits the bill. There are many plants to choose from, but candytufts and *Phacelia tanacetifolia* could provide the main sources of nectar; there is room for experimenting in order to find the best species.

After flowering, collect seeds from the annual plants that you like best. In the autumn, take out all the old plants and, over the winter, hoe the soil to kill off any unwanted seedlings, saving any that you recognise and want to keep. Meanwhile, sow the collected seeds into 9cm (3in) pots. Do this randomly, so there are a few different species to each pot. Place the pots in a well-lit, cool, frost-free place.

In the spring, after the last frosts, place the young clumps of annuals out into the raised bed about 40cm (15in) apart. Each year, buy the seeds of a few new species to add to the pots, but remember always to choose wild species rather than cultivated varieties, as they will be better nectar plants.

An exotic annual meadow.

BUTTERFLY FAMILIES

When starting to indentify butterflies, knowing which family the butterly belongs to is a good start. This section begins that acquaintance; later there is more detail, to differentiate between a number of species similar to each other. There are seven families of butterflies in Britain, but two of these have only a single representative, both very rare. They are the Swallowtail (Family *Papilionidae*) and the Duke of Burgundy (Family *Riodinidae*); neither is commonly seen in gardens. That leaves five families:

Family H*esperiidae*, the Skippers

There are eight skippers in Britain, five of which are known as golden skippers for their bright orange-brown colouration. Only three of these, though, are regularly seen in gardens: the Large Skipper (the most frequent garden visitor), Small Skipper and Essex Skipper. All three lay their eggs on grasses. They habitually sit with their forewings and hindwings at different angles. These are the most moth-like of butterflies.

Family P*ieridae*, the Whites and Yellows

There are seven British species of this family, five of which are commonly seen in gardens and one only occasionally. At rest, they are easy to tell apart, but in flight some can be difficult to identify. The infamous Cabbage Whites (Large and Small White) are part of this family, as is the Green-veined White. The other two regularly seen in gardens are the Brimstone and the Orange-tip. The Clouded Yellow is more rarely seen.

Family L*ycaenidae*, the Hairstreaks, Coppers and Blues

These butterflies are among the most active insects in the garden. They are small and swift. Many of them have a metallic sheen to their wings. If your garden is next to wild grassland, then the Small Copper and the Common Blue might be visitors. The Holly Blue is commonly seen in gardens. Most of the male blue butterflies are actually blue, but there is an exception: the Brown Argus. The hairsteaks are known to visit gardens, but four of them spend most of their lives in the treetops and are rarely seen.

Family N*ymphalidae*, the Vanessids and Fritillaries

The 'Aristocrats', as they used to be known, are the best known and loved of garden butterflies. The four most familiar species predominantly lay their eggs on nettles. They are the Small Tortoiseshell, the Red Admiral, the Peacock and the Comma. The Painted Lady is common in some years, and thistles are its main foodplant. These butterflies appear to have only four legs, the first pair of legs being non-functional.

FROM TOP *The Large Skipper,*
The Small White,
The Common Blue.

FAR LEFT *The Small Copper.*
LEFT *The Small Tortoiseshell.*

GARDEN BUTTERFLIES

The fritillaries are superficially similar in appearance. They have a rich orange-brown background colour to their wings, overlaid with a chequered pattern. They are some of the fastest declining of British butterflies and unlikely to be seen in a garden unless it lies close to one of their specialised habitats. The exception is the Silver-washed Fritillary, which sometimes leaves large open woodland to visit buddleia bushes in the garden. In flight the Comma can look like a fritillary.

Family *Satyridae*, the Browns

There are 11 species of browns in Britain and, depending on the part of the country, five or six can be seen visiting gardens. They all lay their eggs on grasses.

All the browns have false 'eyes' – dark marks on the outer edges of the wings. These help confuse birds and other predators about the position of the head and tempt them to peck at the wings instead. Most of the browns are actually brown, many with orange patches laid over the brown background. The exception is the Marbled White, which has black and white markings.

ABOVE *The Silver-washed Fritillary*
RIGHT *The Meadow Brown*
BELOW *The Marbled White*

Chapter Two

Into the Shade

I have followed many butterflies. Many, if not most, species will turn back as soon as they reach an area of shade. Hedges and trees form a barrier to some species; others are happy to hop over. Some species of butterflies, like the Green-veined White, will move quite happily through areas of dappled sunlight. The female likes to lay her eggs on the seedlings of garlic mustard and other crucifers of moist, warm, semi-shaded places. But if you notice a butterfly dive into a thick hedge, or into the depths of a big clump of grasses, it is most likely to be a moth.

This back garden-land of light and shadow is, in effect, an enormous convoluted woodland

Imagine you can hover over your neighbours' gardens. To progress from garden to garden, you make for the areas of light, following shafts of sunlight through the more heavily shaded spots to open areas above the flower borders and ponds. This is how I imagine the Green-veined White experiences the world (with the addition of great wafts of billowing scent).

Speckled Wood.

edge, with hedges and shrubberies and specimen trees that never grow close enough to turn into real woodland. There are three butterflies that do well in this semi-shady environment: the first we have met, the Green-veined White, then there is the Speckled Wood and the Holly Blue.

THE SPECKLED WOOD

The Speckled Wood is a member of the brown family. There are three broods a year in the South and two in Scotland. In the South, the broods overlap so that it may be seen from early April till October, although I find that it is most often seen in April and May, and from late July till October. This species has expanded its range in recent years and may now be found in maturer gardens. The main ingredient that would encourage it to stay and breed is wild grasses. Its natural habitat is the edges of woods, where dappled sunlight falls upon these species. Wood false brome is an attractive grass and one of the favoured foodplants of the Speckled Wood. It is a plant to grow thickly under shrubs and trees, its broad blades enhancing an understory planting of bulbs and herbaceous plants.

In many gardens, the shrubs and trees are inherited from the former owner of the house. If you are starting from scratch, however, you can put them where you want. There are a number of trees and shrubs that are of direct benefit to butterflies, but the suntraps and shelter they create are perhaps the greatest boon. Thus if you have a limited area, place them on the north side of your garden. This way, you will be making the best use of the sunlight and not casting shadows across nectaring areas. (You have to hope that the neighbour to the south of you is not thinking the same thing.)

Native trees, with the addition of a few exotics like buddleia, provide the most benefit to butterflies. But although there are about 60 species of native butterfly there are 2,500 moths; to take one example, twice the numbers of moths use birch as their foodplant as there are species of butterfly in Britain. Moths are a crucial element in the food chain and if

Wood false brome.

The Puss Moth caterpillar on a young aspen.

you are planting trees and shrubs it is important to consider the 'night shift'. Birch, willow, hawthorn, aspen and oak are some of their best foodplants, though every native species of tree in Britain probably has a moth that uses it specifically.

There are a number of butterflies that use trees and shrubs as foodplants, although only three trees will generally be much used in gardens. They are alder and purging buckthorn, and holly. Holly and ivy are the major foodplants of the Holly Blue.

THE HOLLY BLUE

When you see a blue butterfly dashing through your garden above head height it will most likely be a Holly Blue. This butterfly has two broods a year, the first laying eggs on flower buds of the holly and sometimes the leaf tips of male holly trees. The second brood uses the flower buds of ivy. They occasionally also use spindle, dogwoods and gorse.

In some years, there will be large numbers of Holly Blues, then the following year they are hardly seen. A small parasitic wasp is thought by some to cause this fluctuation in numbers. It lays its egg inside Holly Blue caterpillars, eventually killing them. When Holly Blues are abundant the wasp population increases and huge numbers of caterpillars are killed. The following year, there are few Holly Blues and so the parasite becomes scarce, allowing butterfly numbers to build. Eventually the butterfly numbers recover so it is abundant again, wasp numbers increase because of this, and the whole cycle starts off again.

CLIMBERS

Ivy is a climber and, as well as being the foodplant of the second brood Holly Blues, provides a last-gasp supply of nectar for Red Admirals in October. Another climber to grow is honey-suckle, which is a nectar plant for moths, but also a foodplant of a scarce butterfly, the White Admiral. The golden hop is a bright version of the native plant and one of the food-plants of the Comma. In areas of alkaline soil, old man's beard gives nectar late in the year.

There are native shrubs that are good nectar plants. For the first butterflies of the year, the catkins of 'sallows' (willows) are important. Later in the year, wild privet and brambles are among the best. The best place to position all the 'butterfly shrubs' is on the south side of a hedge, fence or small shrubbery.

TOP Male Holly Blue.
BELOW Holly Blue female laying an egg on a flower bud.

Golden hop.

One of the fascinating things about visiting butterfly gardens is seeing how the various 'how to create a butterfly habitat' problems are solved differently from garden to garden, using similar but subtly different solutions. This problem-solving can lead to an interest in butterfly habitat creation becoming something of an obsession. A great deal of time can be spent thinking about how soil could be manipulated to encourage plants to grow in a way butterflies like.

THE LIEBERT GARDEN

Tony and Annie Liebert have been developing their butterfly garden in Somerset for the last 25 years. It is a large garden with a wide range of created butterfly habitats.

The area immediately around their house is now a mature garden, with some tall trees, lots of shrubs and island beds surrounded by irregularly-shaped lawns. The overall feel is of a wood with lots of small glades. The trees let in enough light for most of the garden to receive full sun for part of the day, and the butterflies move with the sun.

This is a garden that looks superficially as any garden might. It is only when you examine the details that you realise it is a butterfly garden. For instance, the trees planted over 20 years ago were planted with butterflies in mind. Oak, ash and elms are the tallest, but below the canopy there are wild plums (Red Admiral and Speckled Wood like the rotten fruit), buddleia (the 'wild' variety) and other shrubs that bees like. There are also ivy trees. These are posts that ivy has been trained to grow up. They look like small shrubs and every year Tony finds Holly Blue caterpillars on the flower buds. Honeysuckle can be treated in the same way.

There is a buddleia hedge and two huge, free-standing buddleias, backed by a dense layer of vegetation. Tony thinks the butterflies like this, as it helps create a heat trap.

Down in the island beds, there are many wild flowers growing between the garden flowers. Old-fashioned Michaelmas daisies are a great draw in the early autumn. Two of the beds are full of garlic mustard for the Green-veined Whites. Alkanet proliferates. This is for the small colony of Scarlet Tigers. These moths are day-flying and brightly coloured – scarlet, black and white. They lay their eggs on a wide range of plants. Comfrey and nettles are two commonly used plants, but Tony and Annie find alkanet to be the favourite in their garden.

THE COPPICE

Another form of woodland gardening could copy the coppicing cycle that used to take place in many if not most of British woods. Six of our fritillaries, as well as the Wood White and Duke of Burgundy, were highly dependant on this form of woodland management. They are scarce butterflies today and, though it is unlikely that a garden-sized wood would be any help

FAR LEFT *Ivy post for the Holly Blue.*
LEFT *Garlic mustard beds, ideal for semi-shaded gardens.*

to them, it could be a low-maintenance form of gardening that would attract other butterflies.

In the traditional coppice cycle, a section of the wood would be cut over the winter for timber, fencing, firewood and so on. Trees would be cut down to ground level, leaving only stumps. The next winter, another section would be cut, and so on. When many of our deciduous trees are coppiced they re-grow very quickly: each section could be cut again seven or more years later. There would therefore be a lot of different sections, all at different stages in their regeneration. A newly-coppiced section lets in a lot of light and plants such as violets and cow-wheat increase dramatically. Five of our fritillaries lay their eggs on violets and one on cow-wheat and they followed this violet and cow-wheat explosion from clearing to clearing.

We could apply a version of this coppice cycle to gardens. I have long wanted to make a Butterfly B-wood (on a well-drained site to suit the buddleia). The main bushes would be buddleia and buckthorn – purging buckthorn, which also favours drier conditions, would be the preferred species – with broom and bramble below. A few bullace, blackthorn and birch would add variety. The woodland floor (see below) would be carpeted with bulbs of various sorts, especially bluebell. Other nectar sources would be bugle and the lungwort 'Blue Ensign'. Garlic mustard just sneaks in under its other name, Jack-by-the-hedge. The main grass would be brome (wood false). Near the edges would grow betony and large bird's-foot trefoil.

You could coppice the buddleia every two or three years, and the buckthorn and broom every four or five years. They would need to be cut in sections large enough to allow significant light in to promote re-growth.

The easiest way to make this wood would be to lay down some biodegradable matting. This would kill off the existing vegetation. A thin layer of woodchips could hide the matting. Then, in the autumn, poke buddleia cuttings through the mat into the ground below. Grown like this, buddleia can create a low wood in two to three years. Plant buckthorn, broom and other plants and bulbs through slits in the matting. By the time the material begins to degrade the weed seeds will have disappeared and the trees will be large enough to cast shade, so that only those plants normally found on a woodland floor can thrive – even ones that don't begin with 'B'.

GARDEN BUTTERFLIES

A buddleia wood.

THE WOODLAND FLOOR

Woodland flowers are important to butterflies. Many plants of woodland and semi-shaded places flower early in the year, before the understorey is shaded by a canopy of leaves. This is where the first butterflies come to find their first sips of nectar. Primroses (prime rose – the first rose) and bluebells are followed by red campion.

Under the shrubs of the spiral garden at Ryewater, between rafts of crocus, hundreds of lungworts have been planted. *Pulmonaria augustifolium* 'Blue Ensign' provides a vivid blue contrast to the crocus *C.tommasinianus*. Twenty species or types of violet are grown, and bugle makes another bright splash of blue.

By the time the canopy is closing over, many plants will be flowering in the open parts of the garden and we now go to the south-facing edge of the shrubbery, where heat and nectar are concentrated. Native shrubs for nectar to plant here are broom and wild privet, but it is the non-native buddleia that really draws in the butterflies.

Orange-tip nectaring on bluebell.

Male Brimstone.

Buckthorn and Brimstone

On the first warm days of spring, the male Brimstone is on the lookout, searching and scouring the hedgerows. It is a large butterfly, with durable, sulphur-yellow wings. The male is looking for a female Brimstone. When he finds her, an aerial pursuit takes place, followed by conquest in the bushes. By early May, the cream-coloured female displays the same searching behaviour, but she is looking for buckthorn. Purging – or common – buckthorn and alder buckthorn are shrubs or small trees that are the only foodplants of the Brimstone. After she has mated, a female seeks out one or other of the buckthorns, and she may stay in the vicinity of the chosen bush for some time. She will lay a few eggs, fly away to seek out new bushes, only to return to the same bush to lay more eggs. She looks for buckthorns that grow in sunny, sheltered positions. I once found 23 eggs on one small buckthorn sprig protruding from a mass of foliage. When I investigated the next day, there were only three; something had eaten them. Butterflies are under threat at every stage of their life cycle.

Very few buckthorns growing in suitable situations are not visited: Brimstones must be one of the easiest butterflies to attract to your garden. Specialist nurseries will sell the shrub in various sizes but even buckthorn whips a metre tall will attract investigating females.

Alder buckthorn is found in acidic soils, often in damp situations, while purging buckthorn likes dryer soils. I have both plants growing in the same hedgerow, although the alder buckthorn does not seem as happy as the purging (so-called because the berries were eaten to relieve constipation). However, the Brimstone lays on both with equal fervour. Plant the bush or bushes on the south side of an existing hedge or in any sunny, sheltered situation.

For an interesting experiment you could grow buckthorn in a pot (see photos on next page). Cover the sapling with muslin or mesh to keep out any predators. At the beginning of May, place the pot on a box or an old chair to raise the pot above the ground and take off the muslin cover. Put it in a sunny, sheltered position and wait for the Brim-stone female to lay. You will find her eggs laid on the underside of the leaf tips, looking like tiny milk bottles. As soon as the eggs are laid, replace the muslin cover. You can, of course, tie the muslin around the branch of a bush growing in the ground, but it is easier to observe the development of the caterpillar if you place a pot in a convenient spot.

Within two weeks of being laid, the eggs hatch and the young caterpillars feed on the upper side of a leaf. Look for a partially nibbled leaf and then look along the midrib. The caterpillars rest along this, occasionally stretching out to nibble a bit more of the leaf. The camouflage is wonderful, but once you have got your eye in they are quite easy to spot. At this stage, outside the protection of your muslin tent, many of the caterpillars would be eaten by warblers.

In the wild, the leaf-like chrysalis of the Brimstone is rarely found, but within the protective tent you can see the whole process. Be prepared to release the emerging adult after a couple of weeks – it needs to feed to be ready for the winter hibernation.

TOP *Narrow-leaved everlasting pea. One of the Brimstone's favourite nectar plants. Other butterflies cannot reach the nectar at the base of the narrow-leaved everlasting pea's long flower tube, but the Brimstone has a long proboscis.*
ABOVE *Netted buckthorn.*

1 *Potted buckthorn and laying Brimstone.*
2 *Magnified egg. Laid on the underside of young leaflets, looks like a tiny milk bottle.*
3 *The Brimstone caterpillar indoors.*
4 *The chrysalis resembles a leaf.*

Buddleia

'Buddleja' or 'buddleia'? They keep changing the spelling. This is the heavyweight nectar champion. Margaret Vickery conducts a survey for Butterfly Conservation, asking butterfly gardeners to note the butterflies that visit their gardens and which plants they nectar on. The number one nectar plant is buddleia, almost ten times as popular as the second most popular, the ice plant, *Sedum spectabile*.

When we talk about buddleias we are usually referring to *Buddleia davidii* and its many varieties, hybrids and cultivars. There are other species of buddleias, some of which also make good nectar plants. Before coming to them, however, I would like to consider the popularity of the buddleia and put forward a small challenge to its pre-eminence.

Butterflies, like children, will devour the best first. *Buddleia davidii* flowers from early July onwards, but my own plants – and those I find in the abandoned quarries near where I live – are butterfly-empty at this time. Buddleias in gardens are certainly visited, but it is not until later on in August and September that butterflies take a real interest in their blooms. This is when the vanessids attack the buddleias in force. Why are they the flavour of the month in August but not in July? Could it be that there are other plants that butterflies prefer to nectar on at that time? The last week of July is the high point in my summer meadow. It is full of flowers and there is colour everywhere. At this point, marjoram rules OK. A week or two later and the scene has changed, with tawny grass and seed heads making a meadow of ochres. There are still plants to nectar on but the wild profusion has gone.

Two flowers are yet to reach their peak. They are the small and the Devil's-bit scabious, and throughout August and into September they are the kings in my meadow. A couple of buddleias, visited but not swamped with butterflies, overlook the throngs on the scabious. Why not try growing lots of these two plants next to your buddleias, as a small contest? Make it fair, though: put them in full sun, not in a shady corner.

Painted Lady on scabious.

Buddleia alternifolia.

43

Red Admiral *nectaring on* Buddleia davidii 'White Profusion'

It is possible to have buddleias flowering in your garden from spring to late autumn, although, compared with the free-for-all in August and September, the very early flowering buddleias have few visits from butterflies, mainly because there are not many butterflies about. One of the first buddleias to flower is *Buddleia candida*. It is susceptible to frosts but a good pruning usually sorts this out. *Buddleia alternifolia* flowers in early summer. I have one in my back garden but I have yet to see a butterfly on it. Butterflies may show no interest in a plant in one place yet use it constantly in another. The *alternifolia* at Ryewater is visited regularly. The cultivar of this plant, *Buddleia alternifolia* 'Argentea', has beautiful silver leaves.

The next to flower is *Buddleia globosa*. The butterfly season is beginning to hot up by this

Peacock on Buddleia, nectaring.

time and it gets a few more visits from butterflies than the earlier buddleias. *Globosa* bridges the gap between the early buddleias and the many forms of *Buddleia davidii*.

There are huge number of varieties and cultivars of *Buddleia davidii*, as well as a number of hybrids. As suppliers of nectar, none are probably any better than the ordinary bomb-site buddleia. As far as varieties are concerned, though, *Buddleia davidii* var. *magnifica* is, as its name suggests, magnificent, sporting huge flower heads.

The range of colours available is stunning. A white cultivar often recommended is *Buddleia davidii* 'White Profusion'. This shrub has loads of flower heads, although when it has finished flowering it looks a bit dowdy. *Buddleia davidii* 'Empire Blue' and *Buddleia davidii* 'Dartmoor' would help give a wide range of flowering times, although they will all flower later if cut back in the spring. Consult David Stuart's book *Buddleja* (see Recommended Reading) for an introduction to the huge range available.

There are two other buddleias flowering in the same time span as the *davidiis* that are worth considering: *Buddleia nivea* and the various *Buddleia x weyerianas*.

Buddleia nivea has insignificant flowers (though still attractive to butterflies) but wonderful foliage. In fact, it is often recommended that the flower heads be removed as this improves the foliage. Its usefulness as a nectar plant would then be limited, though. *Buddleia x weyeriana* is a cross between B. *davidii* var. *magnifica* and B. *globosa* and there are six or seven different varieties. These shrubs resemble *Buddleia globosa* but flower in late summer to early autumn.

Flowering later than most is *Buddleia* 'Clive Farrell'. Clive made a hedge of this plant at Ryewater simply by mounding up a 200m (210yd) length of clay soil, covering it in black plastic and poking cuttings through the plastic. The black recycled plastic looks horrible, but it stops all competition from other plants and retains moisture. When the cuttings are well established it can be removed. After just a year, the cuttings in Clive's hedge were tall (1.5m/1yd 60in), bushy and covered in butterflies.

Many buddleias will grow very easily from cuttings simply stuck in the ground like this. It is the way I grow all mine. Not all take but enough do, and there is hardly any effort involved. Make sure there is reasonable drainage in the spot you select or, if you have poor drainage, make a small mound of earth, cover it with a mat of some sort – even an old black polythene bin liner will do – and push the cutting through it into the ground. Only some of the more sensitive buddleias will need to be in pots.

If you are growing a number of different buddleias in a garden situation you will get a lot

BELOW *Cuttings in plastic.* BOTTOM A *year later.*

Large White on Buddleia x weyeriana.

45

of seedlings; these can be dug up and replanted elsewhere. Who knows? One of these hybrids may be the next star of the buddleia world.

At the end of the year, *Buddleia auriculata* provides a late feed for Red Admirals. The flowers are small but scented. Grow this shrub against a south-facing wall, as a frost can knock it back – although it usually re-grows from the roots.

Other shrubs that are worth considering as sources of nectar over the summer are *Escallonia bifida* and various hebes.

In the late summer and early autumn, the feast that buddleia provides is a boon for butterflies that hibernate or migrate southwards. Michaelmas daisies, golden rod and the ice plant, *Sedum spectabile*, are also all flowering, in competing with buddleia. This is the height of the butterfly gardener's year. But even into November there may still be the odd butterfly visiting ivy, or even rotting fruit under the apple tree.

A late summer feast on a blackberry. The marking that gives the Comma its name can clearly be seen.

Chapter Three

The Garden of
Lost Dreams

We all have dreams; some of these are unfulfilled. The Wicker Witch catches these dreams and weaves them into her wicker animals. There are wolves and stags, eagles and hares, a giant auroch. At night the power of the dream is in the wicker animals and they run, howl, soar and roar across the meadow…

This garden is all about recycling. The brash and other wastes of Ryewater are used to create habitat for butterflies. The Wicker Witch does the same – she takes lost dreams and weaves them into life.

The brief behind this design at Ryewater was to find a way of using the garden's waste materials. These are mostly the brash from coppicing, plus grass cuttings from the meadows. A circular pond surrounded by a henge is at the centre of the design.

Pairs of wicker hares, stags, eagles and wolves guard the four entrances. A double row of chestnut poles spiral round the henge, and in each corner is a labyrinth. Each year the brash is piled between the double row of chestnut poles to make a dead hedge, and the walls of the labyrinths are made from grass cuttings. Every year the walls and the hedge get higher and plants start to grow in them. And it here that we welcome all the 'naughty' plants that are usually shunned in the garden: thistles, willow herbs and docks are all given the red carpet, but the most welcome plant is the nettle.

Plan for the Garden of Lost Dreams. At the centre of the pond is a giant Brimstone egg, modelled on the photograph on page 42.

Below *Nettles and wolves. Willow sculptures made by Kim Creswell*

NETTLES AND NYMPHALYDS

Nettles are mean competitors. They grow thickly and quite tall, casting a dense shadow. Only those plants that grow through and over them stand a chance. They like soils rich in phosphates. They also mark where man has been. In the highlands of Scotland you can range for miles over mountain and moor and see not a single nettle, but find a croft abandoned hundreds of years ago and the nettle will be there.

Nettles are also the foodplant of four of the most colourful garden butterflies: the Small Tortoiseshell, the Peacock, the Red Admiral and the Comma. Each has a slightly different approach to the nettle bed. The Small Tortoiseshell female likes the young growth of nettles near the edge of a bed, in a sunny position. This is where she will choose to lay her batch of eggs. There may be 50 or more laid on the underside of the highest leaf of the plant. The caterpillars then congregate in a silken web woven around the topmost leaves. Later they disperse and can be found singly, resting on nettle leaves.

The Peacock female is more likely to lay her batch of eggs on plants near the middle of the nettle bed, which makes them more difficult to get to. She lays her eggs at midday in full sunshine. Peacock caterpillars also spin communal webs.

The Red Admiral lays her eggs singly on the growing tips of young plants. Most are laid in open situations but some are laid in semi-shady spots. When the eggs hatch, the caterpillars make a tent by drawing the leaves' edges together with silken threads.

The Comma also lays eggs singly, on leaf tips, often selecting nettles growing in shady situations. The caterpillars form a silken web on the underside of the leaf.

Numerous moths also lay their eggs on nettles. The Burnished Brass and the Snout are two of the commoner ones.

A number of different forms of nettle are grown at Ryewater. The most popular among human visitors is the golden nettle. It is an attractive plant, especially when young. There are also American giant nettles, purple nettles and stingless nettles.

FAR LEFT When young, the Small Tortoiseshell caterpillars spin a silken web. They are light brown in colour.
LEFT Later, the caterpillars disperse and are found singly on nettle leaves. At this stage, they are black, with varying amounts of yellow markings overlaid.

FAR LEFT Peacock caterpillars have long, black spines, which help differentiate them from a black form of Small Tortoiseshell caterpillars.
LEFT The Comma caterpillar lives in a silken web on the underside of a nettle leaf. As it gets older, it comes to resemble a bird dropping.

FAR LEFT The Red Admiral caterpillar spins itself a tent of nettle leaves.
LEFT The Red Admiral caterpillar.

Butterfly sculpture and golden nettles. In this garden-sculpture the butterfly's body is fomred by a bridge. The wing shapes are planted with golden nettles. Down come butterflies to lay eggs – on a butterfly.

The black form of Small Tortoishell caterpillars on golden nettle.

MAKING YOUR BED

The nettle bed needs to be as far as possible in full sunshine. A sheltered spot is best – against a south-facing hedge or fence would be good. The larger you can make it the better. It could be the place you dump all your grass cuttings, making the bed steeper and higher. As for the nettles, you could buy or collect seed but I am sure somebody would be only too happy to let you dig up a few of their plants. Nettles spread by underground runner and will soon fill your bed.

Small Tortoiseshells and Red Admirals like a fresh, young growth of nettles on which to lay their eggs. This is not a problem in the early part of the year but, when second-brood butterflies are out, the nettles are getting old and stringy. Cutting down nettles in mid-to late June is the best way of promoting fresh growth ready for second-brood butterflies in July and August. However, Peacocks – which usually have only one brood, early in the year – need the nettles their webs are on. If you keep an eye open you can avoid destroying webs, and anyway only a quarter to a half of the bed need be cut. The cuttings can be left in place and the caterpillars will crawl off onto fresh plants. I generally cut my patch with a strimmer but a scythe would be more precise – besides being good for the stomach muscles.

There is another group of plants that would be appropriate here: the thistles. Some thistles grow high enough to have their heads above the nettles but you could also aim to keep some areas free in order to increase the edge habitat and encourage the Small Tortoiseshell to lay. In these bare or edge areas of the nettle bed thistles and other tall plants could be grown.

ABOVE *Painted Lady caterpillar.*

Thistles are good nectar plants, and they are also the foodplant of the fifth nymphalid that is likely to come into the garden (it seems appropriate to have the complete set in one place). The Painted Lady has a number of different foodplants but the thistle is always preferred. Musk and spear thistle are biennual but easy to raise from seed – a few plants could be grown in seed trays and added to the nettle bed each year. Scotch and woolly thistles would also work well here, as would other tall biennuals such as common mullein and teasel.

If you make a meadow you are likely to strip topsoil from it (see Chapter 5). You could use this removed fertile soil to make a small south-facing bank. As in the Garden of Lost Dreams, you could then plant this bank up with more of the species that are usually unwelcome. A hedge of brambles, for instance, could be grown on the north side, providing both nectar and shelter.

This shelter and degree of shade might also encourage the Comma to lay. The nettle is not the only foodplant of the Comma. In the 19th century she was more likely to lay her eggs on hop if she finds it. With the demise of the hop-growing industry the Comma switched to using nettles as her main foodplant, but she will still use hops. The hop is related to nettles and, like nettles, will attract a host of insect life in addition to butterflies. Plant it on your bank and it will scramble through the brambles. In the autumn the bramble hedge will be decorated with garlands of hop seed-heads.

In this area we have created a patch for 'naughty' plants; by growing another group of plants, brassicas, at the front of the bed we could create an area for 'naughty' butterflies.

THE CABBAGE WHITES

The Large and Small Whites are well-known to vegetable gardeners. Their main foodplants are cultivated brassicas, although they will also lay on nasturtium. It would be interesting to know the range of these insects before man started growing the wild cabbage, *Brassica oleracea*. In Britain and Europe it is a scarce plant, found on sea cliffs. These butterflies have a number of foodplants, however, and charlock (this is another to grow in the nettle bed), sea kale and mignonette are all found in the wild.

The cabbage whites have followed the domestic cabbage and other brassicas all round the world. In North America they are known as the 'cabbage worm'. Yet the Large White is a handsome insect, and they are both welcome in my garden (I don't grow cabbages). The gardener has a friend in a parasitic wasp that injects its eggs into the butterfly larvae. The wasp larvae then eats the caterpillar from the inside. A huge proportion of caterpillars may be killed in this manner. Yet the numbers of cabbage whites can still be immense, with large migrations of both insects coming from the continent to supplement home-grown stock.

ABOVE *The Large White.*
LEFT *Caterpillars and eggs on cabbage.*

PREVIOUS PAGES *Aerial photos of Ryewater Nurseries.*

Ryewater Nurseries

Since he was a boy, Clive Farrell has had a fascination with moths and butterflies.

In 1981 he opened the London Butterfly House, a tropical greenhouse maintained for tropical butterflies. Since then he has built several more. During the building of the London Butterfly House he met Miriam Rothschild – pioneer in the art and science of creating meadows – and they became friends. They collaborated on the book, *The Butterfly Gardener.*

At his home in Dorset, Clive has been slowly changing over 40ha (100ac) of land from an almost butterfly-free zone into a butterfly paradise. All the land is managed, designed or manipulated for the benefit of butterflies and moths and other wildlife.

One of the great spurs that encouraged him to create habitat for lost butterflies was the discovery of a schoolboy's project. As recently as the early 1960s a local schoolboy had studied the butterflies around Ryewater and had noted good colonies of Marsh Fritillary, Small-boarded Fritillary and Duke of Burgundy. All these butterflies have since disappeard, and are not only scarce or very rare in Dorset, but also nationally.

One of the first projects Clive undertook was the creation of the R-field, in honour of his wife Rajna. The world's largest 'R' is written across the landscape in hedges and banks. The 9ha (23ac) field had been 'improved' and was botanically very poor, with a few species of agricultural grasses and a bit of clover. Now there are over 200 species of plants and huge numbers of butterflies.

Since then, many projects for butterflies have been undertaken. Ivan Hicks and myself help with the design. Trevor, Simon and Denise Cuff do the earth moving and planting. Leslie Pattenden, a keen and knowledgeable entomologist, is head gardener and manages all the formal gardens.

Although its scale is large, this Dorset site contains ideas that may be used in the smallest garden.

UP THE WANDERERS

With the exception of the Speckled Wood, all the butterflies we have talked about so far are wanderers, spending large parts of their lives as adults, moving from place to place. Native populations of the Large and Small White are supplemented by influxes of continental insects. Other butterflies annually migrate across continental Europe. The Painted Lady originates in the Mediterranean but reaches Britain every year. It travels northwards, breeding as it goes. This northward migration may not be completed by the insect that started the journey but by its progeny. Painted Lady adults, eggs, larvae and chrysalises are unable to survive British winters and the population here depends upon fresh immigrations each year.

A similar tale, with minor differences, can be told of the Red Admiral and the Clouded Yellow, although they are more capable of over-wintering in Britain. The Clouded Yellow and the Painted Lady, instead of wandering, will settle in one place for a time.

The home-grown stocks of the cabbage whites wander around the countryside and gardens, on the look-out for foodplants and nectar. They can cover considerable distances. Their close relatives, the Green-veined White, the Orange-tip and the Brimstone, are local nomads, following hedgerows and gardens, seeking out nectar and foodplants. The same is true for the Holly Blue.

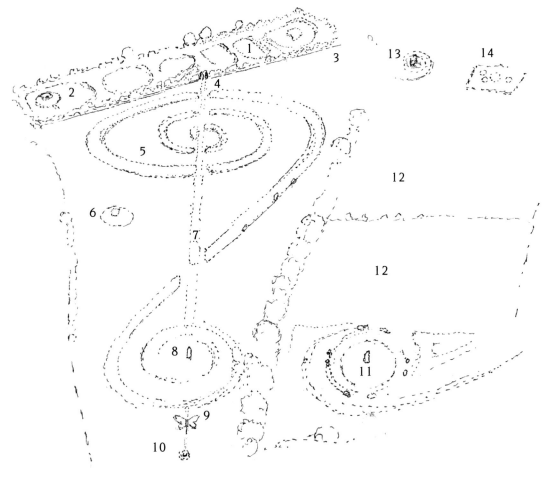

RYEWATER

KEY TO FEATURES MENTIONED IN THE TEXT

1 Bramblearium
2 Gnome's house
3 Buddleia hedge
4 Dragon's gate
5 Sleeping dragon
6 Seaside garden (Island of Dreams)
7 Dragon path
8 Dragon stone
9 Nettle butterfly
10 Ogre's chair
11 Garden of Lost Dreams
12 Bird fields
13 Spiral garden
14 Prison garden
The R-field is shown at top right of photograph on previous page.

The Clouded Yellow. Each year, Clouded Yellows migrate northwards from southern Europe. In some years, large numbers cross the channel. The Clouded Yellow is occasionally found over-wintering, as a caterpillar.

Comma nectaring on scabious.

The four nymphalids – the nettle feeders – also wander the countryside. The Small Tortoiseshell and Peacock males are morning travellers. In the afternoon they establish territories, waiting for females. The Peacock male you see this afternoon in your garden will probably not be the same one you saw yesterday afternoon.

The Comma males are more likely to keep to the same afternoon territory. They find a suitable hot spot – often where two paths or ways meet – and dive out to intercept anything that could be a female. This might be a stick thrown into the air or any dark object sailing past. There is one small spot in my garden that is occupied spring and late summer, year after year after year. The place faces west and is at the junction of two paths. It is hot in the afternoon sun. Without fail, twice a year, the same square half-metre of ground is occupied by a male Comma. I am tempted to think of it as the same individual, so regularly is the same spot chosen, but of course it is a new butterfly each time. The individual that claims the place will return each afternoon for a week or so, and then fade away.

Later in the year, they might all stay for a while in one area if there is a plentiful supply of nectar.

This wandering lifestyle is the main reason why these butterflies are the commonest garden butterflies. They come for the rich sources of nectar. But other species of butterfly are real stay-at-homes. Some are restricted to tiny pockets of land where their foodplants grow. Others will move short distances to similar habitats nearby. The commoner of these species, in warm years especially, will often come into gardens to nectar. Without the right foodplants they will only be visitors and soon return to their favoured meadow or wood environment. But it is possible to create habitats for some of these butterflies which will encourage them to stay in the garden. These are the butterflies that are the subject of the next section.

Part Two:
Meadow Butterflies

Chapter Four

Down the Garden Path

There is a moth, a day-flying moth, called the Six-spot Burnet. It has six bright red spots on each forewing, set against a green-black background. Large, black, clubbed antennae give it a comic appeal. For me it is the clown of the meadow. It likes warm, sheltered grassland with lots of nectar and plenty of its foodplant, bird's-foot trefoil. The bright colours of the adult and the caterpillar tell predators 'watch out, I am poisonous'.

Another special feature of this moth is that it lives in colonies. What this means is that the individuals of a group of Six-spot Burnets live their entire life cycle in one patch of habitat.

The spiral path at Ryewater.

Some individuals may wander and find other Six-spot colonies or patches of habitat to their liking, but the bulk of the colony remains on its home patch. There are advantages in staying put: if the type of habitat you need is unusual or scarce then finding another as suitable in your short life span may be difficult; you are also more likely to meet a mate within the existing colony and be able to pass on your genes.

This particular burnet likes warm grassland, where bird's-foot trefoil is not smothered by the grasses, and where there are also some taller plants or grasses for the caterpillars to climb. They do this when they are ready to pupate, forming a cocoon high on a grass or plant stem.

There is a colony of burnets in the Spiral Garden at Ryewater. The path – which forms the spiral – is made from chalk rubble. For a few years the path remained white chalk, in which individual plants of horseshoe vetch, bird's-foot trefoil and other chalk-loving flowers were planted.

LEFT *Six-spots mating.*
ABOVE *The caterpillar is brightly marked.*

Six-spot cocoon.

The first years of the path.

Soon, fine grasses moved in and now the path is mown once every week or so during the summer. The chalk plants, especially the medicks and vetches, like this regime and grow thickly in the sward. Because the grass is kept short the ground is warmed quickly by the summer sun and this heat is then radiated back out.

Fresh new growth of trefoil leaves in a warm environment is irresistible to Six-spot females and down they come to lay their eggs. Some of these eggs and the caterpillars escape the lawn mower but they still need a grass stem to pupate. They do this by crawling off the path and climbing a stem in the tameflower meadow nearby.

The spiral path is in fact a spiral meadow. The well-drained chalk rubble does not turn into a mud bath in the winter, even though it is in constant use. Other substrates such as fine gravel could also be used to create both a good walking surface and a superb place for butterfly plants to grow. The key to success is making sure the path is well drained.

Butterfly Colonies

Like the Six-spot Burnet, the majority of Britain's butterfly species live in colonies. Some species are highly colonial, hardly moving from their own small patch of grassland (see Small Blue, Chapter 7). Other species will move short distances to adjoining habitats (see Fritillaries, Chapter 2). Some colonies of butterflies will occupy whole hillsides; others are found on top of a group of trees.

Large Skipper males rocket skywards, chasing rivals till they seem the merest specks. Silver-washed Fritillaries glide by in a golden blur. Meadow Browns, Ringlets and Marbled Whites bob and weave through the long grasses. All these colonial butterflies are masters of the air and do not stay in one spot because of an inability to fly well. Although some individuals within the colony may stray – especially during hot weather – the bulk of the colony stays within its home range. Some species are particularly sedentary and take years to colonise new habitat. Others have individuals within the colony that rapidly colonise new habitat if it is suitable. Two butterflies from this latter group are the Common Blue and the Brown Argus.

In the southern half of Britain both these butterflies are double brooded (bivoltine) and are seen twice a year. Further north they only emerge once a year (univoltine). The individual

BELOW *Common Blue female with extensive blue scales on her upper wings.*
CENTRE *Common Blue female with fewer blue scales.*
FAR RIGHT *There are no blue scales on the upper wings of the Brown Argus.*

adults of both species only live for a short while – maybe a couple of weeks – but this is enough time to mate and lay eggs. The caterpillar develops quickly in midsummer, pupates, and the second brood is flying by August. The caterpillars of the second brood over-winter as caterpillars and pupate in the spring, and the first butterflies of the New Year are flying by early May.

In the South there are many wild sites where only the second brood is regularly record-ed; this suggests that either the first brood is tiny and not seen, or that each year the site is recolonised by the odd first-brood butterfly or later by a number of second-brood butter-flies. Probably both are happening. It is members of the second brood that we have the best chance of enticing into the garden, where they might form a new colony.

The Common Blue likes the same sort of habitat as the Six-spot Burnet. It too lays its eggs on bird's-foot trefoil and other vetches. In long grassland the Common Blue is found in ones and twos but in large areas of fine, sparse grassland it can be counted in the hundreds. The male's upper wings are a beautiful violet blue. The females are more diverse. Some are a uniform brown with a fringe of orange spots. Others have varying amounts of blue on their upper wings.

The Brown Argus, both male and female, is superficially similar to the brown form of the female Common Blue but once you get your eye in they are not too difficult to tell apart. The word I use to describe the difference is 'smart'. The Brown Argus, especially when newly emerged, looks smarter than the Common Blue female. The upper wings are a uniform brown; in contrast the Common Blue's upper wings usually, though not always, have some blue. The way to be sure, however, is to look at the underwings (see below). Both species have a series of spots that look like black and white fried eggs. The forewing of the Common Blue has a 'fried egg' close to the body; the forewing of the Brown Argus has not. Sometimes at rest, though, with wings closed, the back wing can sneak forward and cover these spots.

I have a special affection for the Brown Argus: it was the first uncommon butterfly to move into my meadow, in the early 1990s. The foodplant of the Brown Argus is rockrose and the butterfly used to be found mainly on chalk and limestone downland. Then in the mid 1990s there was a sudden expansion of its range. It is thought that the warm summers of the early part of that decade enabled the Brown Argus to move into other habitats where it used annual cranesbills as its foodplants. My Brown Argus must have been part of that expansion.

Even more than Common Blue, it is the second brood only that is recorded on many nature reserves and other butterfly sites. In my own meadow I hardly ever see the first brood but there are always a few second brood. This suggests that the Brown Argus is capable of

FAR LEFT *The Common Blue forewing has a 'fried egg'*
close to the body.
LEFT *The forewing of the Brown Argus has none.*

colonising new habitat very quickly: we can try to exploit this in our gardens, where butterflies from the second brood may be occasional visitors.

Gravel path with mounds for butterfly plants on each side of the path.

THE HOT PATH

Both the Common Blue and the Brown Argus like short, sparse grassland where their food-plants may grow over bare patches of ground: the garden path can simulate this habitat. The advantage of the gravel path in particular is that it is well drained and will warm up quickly in the sun. Even plants overhanging the gravel will be growing in a warm micro-climate. There are several ways to turn your path into a very good butterfly habitat.

A garden path must be capable of taking a lot of foot traffic: we need to lay down a hard-wearing material. Gravel, chalk, oolite or hardcore chippings could all be used. The more free-draining the path the harder it will be for plants to get a foothold: the material needs to hold some moisture. Chalk and oolite will do this. Gravel may need some soil mixed in but, given time, this will also arrive by itself.

First mark out the route, then dig away any topsoil – it might be spread into the flower border on either side of the path, or put onto your veg patch. A mat could then be laid down to keep soil right out. The path's edges need to be lined to prevent the richer soils creeping back onto the path. This needs to be an effective barrier. It could be done with low paving curbs or by turning up the underlying mat. Then lay down a layer at least 15cm (6in) thick of the material you have decided upon. It could be a combination of materials.

With gravel, you might keep the central walking area free but mound up other materials at either side of the path. Rockrose and cut-leaved cranesbill, foodplants of the Brown Argus, could be grown on these mounds (see illustration below). All the plants you might grow will be covered in Chapter 7. These foodplants will be growing over baking gravel and, since butterflies like warmth, egg-laying females will find them particularly attractive.

If you are going for a mown path, you could sow with just a couple of plants – bird's-foot trefoil and a fine grass like sheep's fescue, for example. If the path will be used a lot, harder-wearing grasses might be preferred, but they can also be sown later into any bare patches

Section through path.

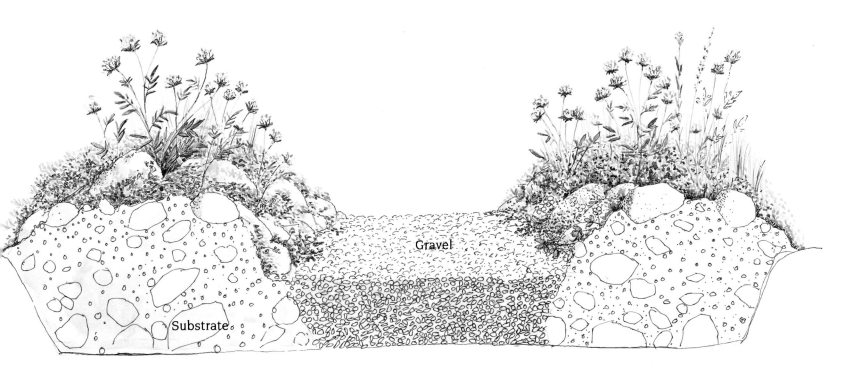

that develop. And remember that, as far as butterflies are concerned, bare patches are no bad thing. Other plants could be introduced as plugs or restricted to pots buried in the gravel. It will take a while for sheep's fescue to grow long enough to warrant cutting; meanwhile the bird's-foot trefoil will be developing nicely. Some patches of thick trefoil near the edge of the path could be left to grow. It is the newly-sprouting leaflets that the female Common Blue likes and if small patches of this vetch are left uncut in June and mid-August to early September this gives the caterpillars a greater chance.

Where is the path leading? To the meadow at the bottom of the garden, of course.

Chapter Five
The Wildflower Meadow

One of the best and quickest ways to create a wildflower meadow is to put the plants on a strict diet. The vigorous plants that need a rich diet give up and go away, leaving the plants you want to keep without any competition. Do this by removing their food – that is, by stripping off the topsoil, the top layer of earth.

Morning in the meadow

The stripped areas of the Sleeping Dragon (see page 129) are full of interesting plants. The topsoil banked to the left of the picture is dominated by tall grasses.

Soil

The richer the soil in a meadow, the fewer plant species there will be. In rich soils the sward tends to be dominated by a small number of very robust species. These not only dominate other species because of their height, but also elbow out other plants at ground level. In general, the deeper the topsoil the higher the plants grow, and there will not only be fewer species, but also fewer individual plants.

Many of the wildflower meadows made over the last decade or so have reverted to patches of long grass because the fertility of their soils is too high. At first, the newly-created meadow does well, with ox-eye daisies and a few other plants putting on a good display, but over three or four years the flowers gradually decrease and docks and coarse grasses take over. By lowering the fertility we reduce the competition from these coarse species. This makes more sense if we consider the way soils and their different characteristics develop.

When the glaciers retreated after the last ice-age, areas of Britain must have resembled a huge quarry, with rocks strewn about and no topsoil. Only certain plants could tolerate these stressful conditions.

As the average temperature rose, a wider range of plants moved in from southern Europe and the natural succession – from bare ground to high forest – cloaked most of Britain with trees. In the process, dead vegetation created the humus we find in our soils today.

Even now, most pieces of land left long enough will turn from bare rock to grassland to scrub to high forest. We can halt this succession at the grassland or meadow stage by cutting the sward. This prevents any taller plants from taking over. However, it would be a mistake to think of the meadow as a 'frozen frame' because, over time, new species move in. The type of plants that will do this depends to a certain extent on the underlying soil.

Different plants are suited to different soils. Soils are usually classified according to the proportions of clay, sand and loam they contain. These different kinds of particles determine how well drained a soil is. Sandy soils are usually well drained, whereas clay soils are apt to hold water, and loamy soils lie somewhere between the two. Since the nutrients that plants need come from minerals dissolved in water, clay soils are potentially richer than sandy ones, where nutrients are quickly leached away. To enrich sandy soils, gardeners recommend digging in plenty of organic matter or humus. We want to do the *opposite* and give the plants a hard time.

Calcareous soils are also generally well drained, and can become acidic when the calcium carbonate is leached out of them. This usually happens in deeper soils, where the limestone or chalk is further from the surface. Areas of gorse on chalk downs can indicate where this has occurred.

There are other chemicals that affect the fertility of the soil and these are the major nutrients: phosphate, potassium and nitrogen. Fertile soils for growing vegetables have plenty of these, and we use good farmyard manure to maintain high levels of these elements in our productive soils. Conversely, phosphate levels have been found to be low in some of the best ancient meadows and these low levels may be the most important factor in maintaining these meadows. When we remove topsoil we instantly lower the phosphate level.

Nitrogen can be a problem, as legumes are capable of 'fixing' atmospheric nitrogen back into the soil. Bacteria living in the root nodules of plants such as clovers are involved in this process, which is why farmers sow clovers into their pastures and why, if possible, we want to avoid them. Desirable legumes, such as birds-foot trefoil, also fix nitrogen, but the butterfly meadow could not do without them. Even rainfall may have a high nitrogen content in some areas. Every soil is different and what may affect one soil adversely may not so affect another.

The soil of some ancient meadows is reasonably fertile but these meadows are managed by cutting for hay in June or July, and then livestock graze the aftermath until February. This regime prevents coarser plants from becoming dominant.

The main part of the butterfly meadow is best cut in October, or even after the first frosts. This allows a greater range of plants and butterflies to complete their life cycles, but also means that coarser and more invasive plants have greater potential to smother or shade-out lower-growing species. If the soil fertility is really low, the vegetation will be too sparse for this to be a problem. Removing topsoil achieves this degree of infertility.

A new road was built not far from where I live. Deep cuttings had to be made through a hillside. The subsoil and rocks that were removed were used to fill in a disused reservoir. The cutting was then coated with topsoil and sown with a wildflower mixture. The same mixture was sown on the reservoir site. You can guess the rest of the story. A few years on, the cutting is rather a plain, though not unattractive, stretch of grassland. The reservoir site is magnificent.

There are other methods of reducing soil fertility. One of the main ones is grazing – or

The former reservoir covered with bird's foot trefoil.

mowing and removing the cuttings – without replacing any nutrients. Studies suggest that this method could take from 10 years on lighter soils to a 'lifetime' on heavier soils to have any appreciable effect. Reducing fertility by stripping, or burying, the topsoil is a much quicker and more effective method.

There are some soils that will produce highly attractive meadows without any removal of topsoil. They are usually very well drained, such as chalky or sandy soils. But even on this kind of ground, a further range of plants can successfully compete and then attract butterflies if the topsoil is removed. Stripping away topsoil with a spade is hard work and the tendency is to say, 'I'm sure that's enough'. But the longer a meadow takes to develop because of thin, infertile soils, the better it will be in the long run. A meadow that is tremendously colourful in the first year is likely to progressively deteriorate.

The thinner the soil the more plants you can grow per square metre. So if your meadow is going to be small – and there is no reason why even a couple of metres square cannot be highly attractive, particularly if linked to path mounds – then I would reduce the fertility as much as possible. There is further information about very low fertility in the next chapter. If you have more room, then you could vary the depth of the soil, going from thin soils to deeper soils. There is a role for deeper soil: certain of the grasses that grow in them are important for butterflies (see Chapter 6).

Creating your meadow

In a garden, a meadow will generally have to be on the small side, although the bigger it can be made the more likely it is to attract permanent colonies of the commoner meadow butterflies. It is difficult to give a minimum size, as every site is different and each species has different requirements. For instance, if you live near an area where meadow butterflies are found, your small meadow could become an extended part of their habitat. Even small patches of grassland may encourage one or two species to colonise. Some species, like the common Blue, may discover your area each year and supplement any home-grown individuals. To attract a wide range of butterflies to colonise, however, an area one twelfth of a hectare (fifth of an acre) and over, may be necessary, though if mounds and other features described in this book are incorporated, there will be a chance of success on patches smaller than this. Even very small meadows will attract wandering butterflies, and other wildlife.

The ideal site should be south facing. It should be sheltered from the north, and, to a lesser extent, from the east and west. A south-facing bank is ideal, but even north-facing slopes can be shaped to include small areas with a southerly aspect.

Shade

The first thing to check is whether there are any trees on the southern boundary that will shade the site for significant periods of the day. If so, the trees may need to be coppiced or pollarded. A hedge on the south side of the site is fine, as long as it does not shade out important areas of grassland: it will be useful in providing shelter.

Coppicing is a traditional method of managing woodland to produce straight poles for building, fencing, firewood and so on. When a tree is coppiced, it is cut down almost to ground level. (The cut is made at an angle, to allow rainwater to run off the stump.) The shoots from the stump will create a tree with three or more trunks, which can themselves be cut back every six to seven years, depending – in this situation – on how much shade is cast.

Many deciduous trees can be coppiced successfully; some, such as sweet chestnut and ash, coppice better than others. Beech is less successful than most. Coniferous trees cannot be coppiced: any shading the southern face of the site will have to be removed, or at least severely trimmed. If the trees you are tackling are of any size, seek expert advice. Some butterflies (especially Gatekeepers) may use coppiced trees to roost on. Pollarding is the same process, except the tree is cut higher up.

Examining the ground

Take a spade and dig a hole to discover what kind of soil you have. There will probably be a layer of dark soil, the topsoil, with a crumbly texture. Below that is the subsoil, which is generally a lighter colour. The subsoil is the layer that lies above the rock or clay.

Now check to see if there is anything of existing interest to wildlife on the site. If this is your garden, then you may already know what there is of value. The site may be an area that has been left to go wild for a number of years and may already have elements that are worth keeping, or it maybe a closely-mown lawn of marginal use to most wildlife and next-to-none to butterflies.

Check to see if there are any pipes or cables underground that could be disturbed by the removal of topsoil and excavation. Take photographs of the site so that you can keep a visual record of your progress.

Research

Before designing a meadow, it maybe worthwhile to investigate any semi-natural meadows in your area. It is possible that there may be some with Site of Special Scientific Interest (S.S.S.I.) status, that will give you a feel for the range of grasses and flowers found naturally in your district. Remember, the British Isles is famed for its diverse geology and a meadow half a kilometre away could support a quite different range of plants to those that yours might contain.

Limestone areas generally have the greatest range of plants and a large number of British plants are only found on the various kinds of limestone, such as chalk and Carboniferous Limestone. Limestones are rocks that contain a large amount of calcium carbonate. The plants that favour these limey soils are called *calcicoles*. Because of the abundance of flowers on limestone sites they are good places to see nectaring butterflies. Another benefit of limestone is its free-draining nature, which helps to create the warmer conditions that butterflies like.

Other soils may also be free-draining, such as those found on heaths. Heathland and moorland soils are acidic, though. It is on acidic soils that plants that dislike lime (*calcifuges*) can be found. *Calcifuges* are also found on neutral soils.

Most soils, especially in areas where people are likely to have gardens, fall somewhere between these two opposites. But it is fun to find out which plants are *calcicoles* and which are *calcifuges*, as it gives you some idea of the underlying geology of an area. Good indicators for limestone are the wayfaring tree, wild privet, dogwood and traveller's joy; if you encounter foxglove, gorse or broom you can guess that the soil is more acidic.

While ancient hay meadows are good places to start to find out about local plant communities, remember they are mown in late July or earlier and are generally without the humps and mounds, bushes and scrub that butterflies like so much.

There is another kind of meadow, which I like to think of as an 'odd corner meadow'. These are odd, small parcels of land that seem to have been forgotten, or are only minimally managed. Quarries, railway cuttings, slag heaps, pieces of land too steep for the tractor to get to, or any fields that are tawny brown in colour during the winter, are all good places to find these half-meadow, half-scrub habitats. You can seek out such sites by using 1:25,000 scale Ordnance Survey maps. Look especially for steep south-facing slopes, indicated by the closeness of the contour lines on the maps. These habitats are often in the process of

MEADOW BUTTERFLIES

Odd corner meadow. This disused quarry displays many features that butterflies like: the trees provide shelter, and heaps and mounds provide micro-climates. A large variety of foodplants and nectar plants are found on the spoil heaps.

turning into woodland but, because many are nutrient-poor, the process takes longer, allowing a diverse range of flowers and grasses to invade the site.

Even in towns and cities there will be odd scraps of land that have developed their own flora and these too can provide inspiration. Abandoned industrial sites, brownfield sites, sometimes have a very rich butterfly fauna.

There is little or no management on these sites, so plants that flower in July or later can set seed. There are often banks and mounds and shelter created by the encroaching scrub, and there is continuity, with little change to the habitat from year to year. All of these factors makes such sites very attractive to butterflies and may give you some good ideas when you come to design your own meadow.

Design

As already mentioned, the size of the site, its geographical position and the type of soil will all affect the kinds of butterflies you can attract to your meadow. However, several features are consistent.

There needs to be:
• a profusion of nectar plants, flowering when butterflies are on the wing
• as many caterpillar foodplants as possible, growing in the right places
• plenty of sun traps and shelter
• contrasts of soil fertility
• sites for roosting and basking

In a wild site, all the above may be present but some distance apart: where the female spends time nectaring might be quite far from where she lays her eggs. In a garden, we have to provide *all* the features, squeezed into a smaller area.

Here are some designs that use the different elements discussed in this book. Every site is different and they are not meant to be followed to the letter. Pick and choose the features that would best suit your own site.

The Meadow Garden

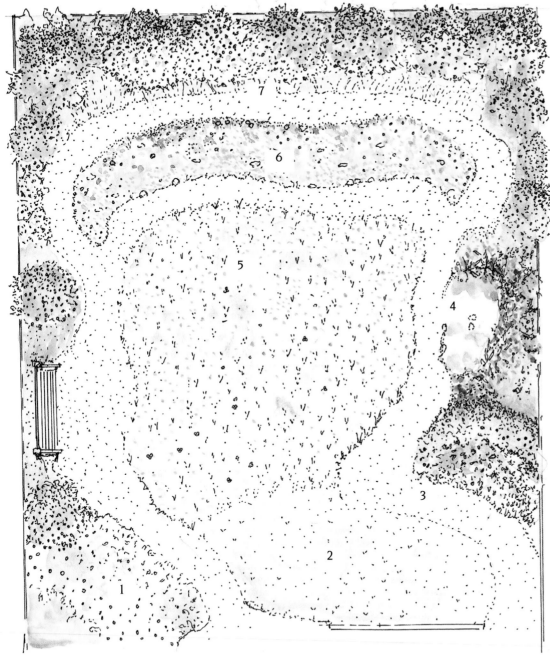

This design could fit into many existing gardens. The top soil is removed from the central part of the garden and is banked on the north end of the garden to make a butterfly bank. The different elements of the design are:

1. Flower border or tameflower meadow.
2. Spring meadow. Cut in early June in time to be used as a lawn during the summer. Early flowering plants to grow here are cowslip and various bulbs, bluebell, wild daffodil and snakeshead fritillary. Sow plenty of bird's-foot trefoil with the grass seed (fine wild grass lawn mixtures are available commercially) as the Common Blue may lay on the newly sprouted leaflets of the mown lawn.
3. Nettle bed.
4. Pond.
5. Wildflower meadow.
6. Butterfly bank (see Chapter 7).
7. Hedgebank.

NORTH

SOUTH

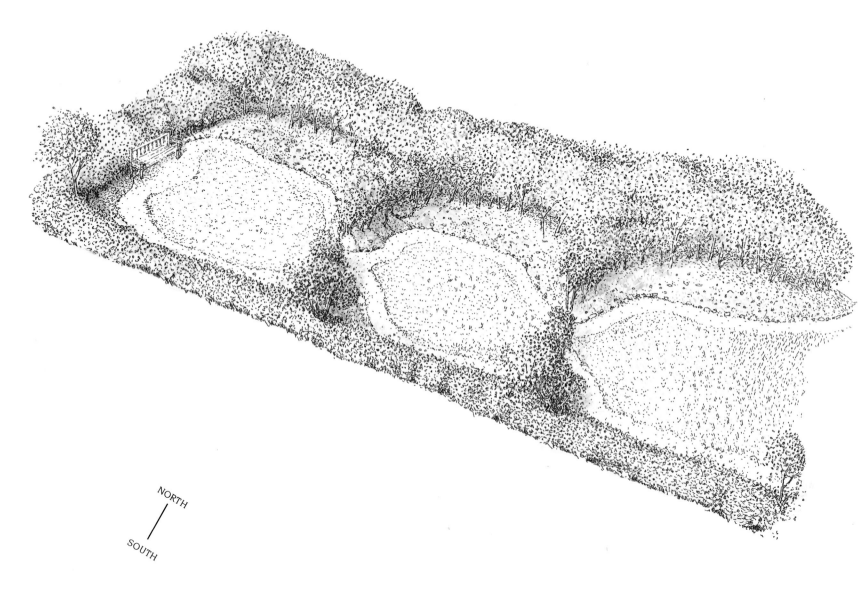

NORTH

SOUTH

The Glades

This design for the larger garden or long thin gardens is a series of glades and is constructed in a similar way to the last design. The top soil is used to create the south facing bank of each glade. There could be a different kind of meadow in each glade. The first meadow could have soils of medium fertility to attract the commoner browns and skippers. The second could be lower in fertility, and the third covered with a layer of substrate. Each meadow would then eventually have a different range of plants. It is important to make sure that the bushes used to separate the glades do not overshadow the banks.

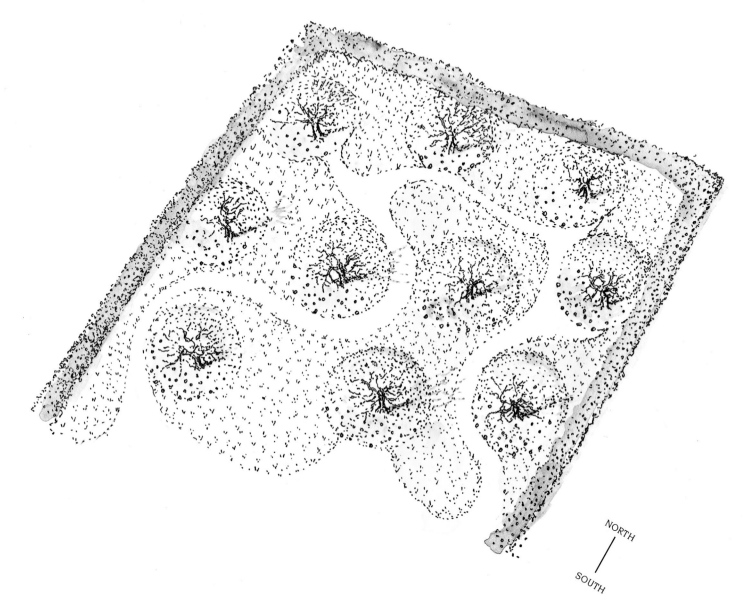

NORTH

SOUTH

The Orchard Meadow

In this design the top-soil is used to make round mounds. Each mound has a fruit tree planted on top. Fruit trees would like the improved drainage of the mounds. The south side of the mound is covered with clay or substrate (see Chapter 7). It would be a good idea to cover the other sides with a layer of subsoil to prevent the germination of weed seeds. The area where the top-soil has been removed is sown with the seed mixtures described later in this chapter. A mown path would give structure to the whole design.

75

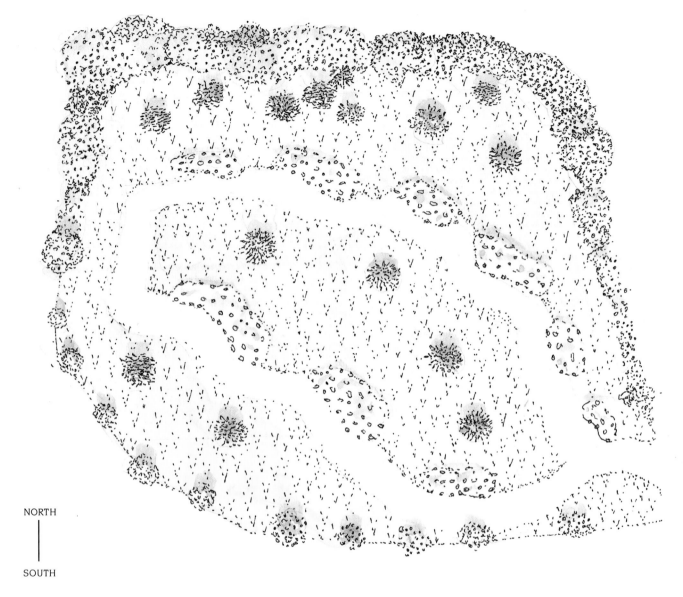

NORTH

|

SOUTH

The Liebert Meadow
This meadow is modelled on Tony Liebert's meadow (see page 124) and would work well on well-drained soils. No topsoil is removed but limestone waste or some form of substrate is used to make a series of mounds. The mounds, after a few years, blend in well with the grassland and can be used to grow a wide range of butterfly plants. Gorse scrub gives the whole meadow a wild and heath-like feel.

Troy Town

One of the great advantages of low-fertility gardening or meadow-making is that any land-forms you make are still discernable at the end of the season. If you used fertile soils to make land shapes they would be lost under long grass by mid-summer. Using infertile sub-soils or substrates you can make any shapes you like, then sow seed of fine grasses and butterfly plants to produce land forms of interest and imagination.

Here is one example (others in Chapter 8) that could be made even in a small garden. Labyrinths have been made to patterns like this for thousands of years and are often called Troy towns. To make this Troy town, the top soil is removed from a circular area and laid all around the circle. Substrates are then used to create the labyrinths walls. In the centre of the labyrinth is a mound with a single tree. The path is either mown grass or gravel. The substrates are sown with all the usual butterfly plants (see Chapter 7). Surrounding the labyrinth is a wildflower meadow

The topsoil that was removed and piled around the circle is covered in a biodegradable mat and then planted with buddleia cuttings (see Chapter 2) or planted with other trees and shrubs. A buckthorn wood would attract Brimestones.

Digger moving topsoil.

BULDOZER OR SPADE?

Can you get a bulldozer into the garden or area of land to be dug? If not, I hope your back is strong, because digging out topsoil is a lot of work. Mini-diggers can be hired that might alleviate this problem; projects can be as small-scale as you like.

Bulldozing is dramatic: the land turned into a canvas waiting to be painted. A bulldozer can do in a minute what it would take you all morning to do with a spade. A bulldozer driver may quote for a day's work. Although moving tons of soil might look to you like a full day's worth, the driver could be finished by mid-morning, so it's worthwhile making sure that he does everything you need while he is there. Other drivers offer an hourly rate.

There are a number of design features to think about when instructing the driver. These might include: bays and mounds, paths, some highly infertile areas with little topsoil, some moderately fertile areas, a pond perhaps, and a hedge bank. All these features are discussed in more detail in later chapters.

The usual time to sow your meadow area is early autumn, but it is best to bulldoze in mid-summer when the ground is dry. This gives you plenty of time to put the finishing touches to your meadow design before sowing.

In a day a bulldozer and dumper truck could, depending on the nature of the terrain, clear a tenth of a hectare (quarter of an acre) of topsoil. On small sites it is probably best to move all the topsoil in one go. On larger areas, it may be better to clear just part of the ground. When this first area has developed, the experience gained can be put to good use in designing and planting up the next section.

If the site you are designing is flat or close to the water table, you may find that you are just digging a pond. There has to be a way for water to run off the site. On sites with a slope, especially if there is poor drainage, water will run to the lowest point. If you are going to have a pond, this is the best place to build it.

The larger the area you are going to clear, the bigger the mountain of topsoil you will have to deal with. What are you going to do with it? It is possible to sell topsoil but you may need planning permission to do this. Another possibility is to put the soil, if it is a small amount, on your vegetable plot. You could also use it to make mounds. Some of the advantages of making these are listed in the panel below.

1. You will not have to get rid of the topsoil (and hiring a lorry to move soil is expensive).
2. By stripping the topsoil you are removing huge numbers of weed seeds as well as nutrients, avoiding the problem of weed seeds sprouting when you are making a meadow.
3. The mound will be a fertile and well-drained area, suitable for a different range of plants to the rest of the meadow.
4. It will give a different perspective to the garden.
5. It creates shelter.
6. Mounds can be covered, on the south side, with various limestones, to let you grow a further range of plants (see Chapter 7).

Step-by-step

The first thing to do is give a clear idea to the bulldozer driver of the result you want. He will probably think you are slightly eccentric by now, so there is no harm in compounding the impression. Show him the illustrations from this book, or draw up your own, to help explain exactly what you require (see the line drawings and photographs in Chapter 7).

Mark out the area of the proposed meadow. Remove the existing sward. If you are going to make shaped mounds it is best to hide grass clumps and other vegetation as far away from the surface of the mounds as possible, as they make shaping the mounds difficult. Then strip the top layer of topsoil down to the subsoil, and either mound up this soil or take it away. The subsoil will generally be lighter in colour, though the subsoils of clay soils tend to be more similar in appearance to the topsoil. Sandy subsoils are particularly good for establishing wildflower meadows. Roughly dig out paths; they can be levelled and shaped with a spade later on.

By this time, the bulldozer driver may be thinking it is time to go home. Before he disappears, make sure that there is nothing else he can do. Is the path flat enough? Does it have a camber? The area that has been dug out will be at a lower level than its surroundings: do you want a graduated change in level? Do you want a pond dug? If the bulldozer has hit rock or rubble, do you want to expose more of it? Do you want to create an area of very low fertility? Do you want areas of deeper soils?

Once the bulldozer has gone, it's time to get out the spade and rake to shape the whole site, harrow the subsoil to create a seedbed, and further develop the paths.

LANDSHAPES

Butterflies like warmth and shelter. Some species like areas of tall vegetation, many others like short, fine grassland. We can shape our ground to reflect these preferences, and we can also shape it to please our eye and to make the meadow accessible.

Paths

It is important to put some thought into where all the paths are going to be, as it may be difficult to change them later. It is best to have two or three main paths with small ones connecting, so that there is access to most of the site without trampling on the flowers. Paths are also useful as a dividing line between habitats – for instance, between areas of short and long grasses. Paths are also your vantage point for observing the butterflies. At the beginning of the year, when the sward is short, you can walk all over the meadow without doing much harm. Later in the year, when the grasses and flowers are taller, walking treads the vegetation down and it can be a week or so before it recovers.

One trick is to dig in some limestone chippings, or other free-draining material, next to the paths at certain vantage points, then plant marjoram. Butterflies love marjoram and will settle on the flowers to sip the nectar, where they can be closely observed from the path.

Making the paths flat and smooth is also important, so you don't have to worry about what your feet are doing. The cheapest option is closely-mown grass and, with the topsoil removed, it may only need mowing a few times a year. If areas of heavy use become muddy during the winter or there are areas prone to waterlogging, gravel and chippings can be spread for fine grasses to grow through. Where wheelchair access is important, you will need to think more carefully about surfacing materials, gradients, path widths, and turning and passing areas.

The Pond

In the meadow area, a larger pond can be considered, rather than the garden pond described in Chapter 1, but many of the suggested plants will be the same. Pond margins and bog areas can support some especially good nectar plants, such as purple loosestrife, ragged robin and water mint. There should be enough room to plant some of the food plants of moths, too. Bulrushes, reeds, bur-reeds and reed sweet-grass are all in this category, though they are invasive and would need to be controlled. To my mind though, this is the place

MEADOW BUTTERFLIES

A path gives structure to the meadow.

where butterflies give way to dragonflies: watching these hawk over a large open pond is one of the most arresting experiences in a wildlife garden.

If there is room, even a small reed bed is a good idea, as it is capable of attracting nesting reed and sedge warblers. You do not see them, but their calls and songs make it very worthwhile.

Areas like this will even give you the opportunity to grow the food plants of butterflies that will never come to your garden. If you become gripped by the butterfly gardening bug, all butterfly plants become special. Here in the marshy area around the pond, you could grow milk parsley (the foodplant of the British subspecies of Swallowtail) and water dock (the foodplant of the Large Copper).

Here are some pond pointers:
• the pond will look more natural if it is sited at the lowest point.
• as far as possible, it should be in full sunlight, preferably without overhanging trees.
• the pond should be stepped, on one side at least, to create different levels for the different requirements of floating, marginal and bog plants.
• shallow sides will support marginal planting, allow wildlife easy access and appear natural.

If space is extensive, it could suit a pond, or even a lake.

• it is useful to have a nearby water source, to conveniently counter the effects of evaporation.
• be aware of safety. If small children are likely to visit regularly, it is probably best to avoid a pond. There are measures you can introduce, such as strong mesh set just below the surface, but it is best to err on the safe side.
• source native species when planting; some non-native species can be aggressive.

On wet sites like Ryewater, just digging a hole produces a pond. On most sites you will have to use a pond liner (though puddled clay is ideal if suitable material is available). After laying the pond liner, cover the whole thing with 5–7.5cm (2–3in) of infertile material – clay or subsoil – and make sure there are no rocks in it.

When you have finished shaping the land and creating a well-raked seedbed, it is time to sow the seeds.

Water dock.

The flowering meadow.

Above *Southern marsh orchid.*
Below *Cowslips: among the first to flower.*

The Flowering Meadow

Most of this book is concerned with creating ideal conditions for butterflies, especially by reducing fertility by stripping off the topsoil. One of the consequences of reducing fertility in this way is the possibility of creating spectacular floral displays relatively quickly. The plants that you introduce to your meadow will wax and wane according to their preferences. Some plants, however, will introduce themselves, and perhaps the most interesting of these are the orchids. One of the most commonly reported phenomena, following topsoil removal, is the invasion of orchids into the stripped area. This has been particularly observed in experiments carried out to create chalk grasslands on former arable land. In my own meadow, heath and common spotted orchids have multiplied. There are also a few early purple, some southern marsh and one bee orchid.

Orchid seed is tiny and each plant can produce thousands of seeds. The seeds may be blown great distances from the parent plant, but there is a far greater chance of the seeds falling on your meadow if there are local orchid populations. Once the seed has landed, it has to come into contact with a mycorrhizal fungus: unlike other seeds, it has no food reserves of its own and the fungus nourishes the plant in the early stages of its life. Some species of orchid are dependant on this fungus all their lives. Orchids grow very slowly and it takes most of the commoner species three to five years to reach flowering size. Some species, like the burnt orchid, can take as long as 15 years.

One of the aims of the meadow-maker is to maintain a good 'show'. It is possible to have a tapestry of flowers from March to September, but it takes a little planning and a little research into the flowering times of plants. Here is a description of the opening times of flowers in my own meadow, created on a south-facing bank. I have listed only those species that provide the main splashes of colour, and of course the times of opening will be different for different parts of the country, but the sequence should be roughly the same.

The season starts in March with primrose and the few bulbs I have planted – wild daffodil, bluebell, crocus, widow iris – but only gets going when the cowslips, bugle and crosswort flower in late April/early May. After this, things really hot up, with the first heath spotted orchids, plus yellow rattle, wild strawberry, salad burnet, buttercups, lady's smock, ragged robin and broom. By mid-May the 'big three' peas, horseshoe vetch, kidney vetch and bird's-foot trefoil, have a large presence, along with the first shy rockroses. Ox-eye daisies provide bright splashes of white against the fresh green of the meadow. At this time of the year the main colours of the flowers are white and yellow. There are exceptions, and they stand out because of it. Milkwort, which is usually blue but can also be pinky-purple or white, is a delicate thing, in contrast to the deep blue columbine (or granny's bonnet), which I transplant from the flower border because it looks so exotic growing in grass. As the season progresses, reds, purples and blues come to the fore. A lot of plants have invaded the bank from the hay meadow, including bush vetch and red clover.

Towards the end of May the heath spotted orchid is joined by the common spotted. It is unusual for both species to grow happily side-by-side but they do so on the bank. The common spotted grows in well-drained as well as damp soils but the heath spotted prefers the latter. The heath spotted is essentially white, but some individuals are almost the same lilac colour as the common spotted. Some of them, I suspect, are hybrids of the two species.

Then rough hawkbit flowers, and it is as if someone has switched on the lights. Rough hawkbit and the widespread cat's ear are like refined dandelions and they make the meadow blaze, but only in the morning as they close up later in the day. They contrast sharply with the large blue flowers of meadow cranesbill. Dropwort is lovely, but only does well in limey soils. In the evening, the quaking grass is a silver shimmer, and luminescent bladder campion a lure to moths. In early June the meadow is bright and sharp. Many of the plants that started opening in May are at their best. Few new plants open and there seems to be a slight pause. Soon a new group of flowers are set to take centre stage.

Corky-fruited water dropwort is a plant found in the South West. It is worth growing for its name alone (as is viper's bugloss, which I try to transplant from the border every year). It is a biennial found at the seaside and will not self-seed in the meadow unless you have sandy, or at least very well-drained, soils. It looks spectacular growing next to sainfoin and dropwort. These provide the old red, white and blue combination that never fails to work.

There are great mounds of field rose in the hedge, which all come from cuttings from one plant. This particular plant produces masses of flowers, as do all the cuttings. In the hedgebank, valerian flower heads sit haughtily on their stalks, while just below them on the bank, grass vetchling peeps out. This is an annual, with brilliant red pea flowers, but until it flowers it looks just like a grass.

At the end of June, betony start to flower. It will not be at its best till the latter half of July, but knapweed and bloody cranesbill are flowering too and the purple-red period has begun. Meanwhile, tall spikes of fragrant agrimony point skyward, while in the hedgebank there is a creamy froth of meadow rue, meadowsweet and hedge bedstraw. There are few new species still to open, but existing species continue to flower, while the grasses are beginning to turn tawny. Meadow cranesbill is blasting blue out into the air and musk mallow, pink. In mid-July, marjoram and field and small scabious join in. Purple loosestrife encircles the pond. Narrow-leaved everlasting pea and fleabane grow alongside spiny restharrow. By early August, in hot years especially, the meadow is beginning to look tired. The dried, burnt umber stalks of heath spotted orchid crumble to dust in your hand. But Devil's-bit scabious provides one last burst of glorious blue.

ABOVE *Rough hawkbit.*
LEFT *The meadow is bright and sharp.*
BELOW *Field rose.*

SEEDS OF BRITISH PROVENANCE

For a number of years botanists have been warning of the danger to our native flora caused by the widespread use of seeds originating elsewhere. Flora Watch reports: 'The majority of wildflower seeds used to create new wildflower grasslands in Britain are sourced from continental Europe, usually eastern Europe, and include fodder varieties and genotypes new to Britain'.

Wild plants are adapted to the region in which they grow and vary genetically from region to region. I would hope that anyone about to make a meadow would try their utmost to make sure that the seeds they use are of British, or even better, local origin. Apart from the conservation issue, there are very good practical reasons for using seeds of local provenance.

Many of the grasses used in meadow mixtures have been developed for their productivity and are more aggressive than wild grasses. Others have evolved in very different environments – some as far away as New Zealand. Seeds of grasses and flowers from your locality are suited to the soil and climate of your locality.

The seed companies that I have recommended in this book go to some trouble to make sure that the seeds they sell in their meadow mixtures are of British origin and, as far as the flowers are concerned, they are all of British provenance. They may sell seeds of continental origin for agricultural use, but this is clearly stated in their catalogues. Their grasses are not all wild, but it is possible to make up your own meadow mix just using native wild grasses. For most people with limited time and resources, this may be the most practical option.

Viper's bugloss and kidney vetch give colour to the meadow in its second year.

There are ways of using seed collected from the area you live in. Although some seed companies offer seed harvested from ancient meadows, the chances of these meadows being close to you are fairly slim. They can also harvest seed for you with a machine called a brush harvester, but the cost of this is quite high. Some botanists would prefer it if the seeds used were all from within a few miles of the meadow to be created, although the practicalities of this make it difficult for the individual to organize.

A method that has had some success is strewing hay. You take hay harvested from a chosen meadow and strew it over your newly-cleared area. The seeds from the hay will fall to the ground, germinate, and you end up with a meadow with some of the same characteristics as the original. The hay should be harvested towards the end of July or beginning of August, when the majority of grass and flower seeds are ripe. Clive Farrell has had great success with this method at Ryewater.

Most seed houses sell wildflower mixes in the proportion of 80% grasses to 20% wildflowers. The species mix is tailored to the type of soil you have: there are different mixes for sandy soils, clay soils, loamy soils and limey soils, as well as general mixes. When I sow a meadow, however, part of me thinks that what is to follow is a war: a war between the flowers and the grasses. Grasses can reach meadow all by itself and, with the least fertility and management, come out on top quite quickly. But many wildflowers are slow developers and they need a head start to gain a real toehold in your meadow. The following method gives them this, although it will only work if you have sufficiently reduced the fertility of the soil: should there still be a lot of topsoil present then the weed seeds in it will germinate.

One of the great advantages of this approach – sowing only a minimal amount of grass seed is – that you will be in a better position to ensure that all the grasses you use are wild. It may be difficult to obtain adequate quantities of the right kind of seed in any one year, but you can carry on sowing flower and grass seed into your meadow for a number of years until the sward closes over. And the meadow is developing well, you could let the grasses arrive by themselves.

Sowing your wild flower meadow

1. After removing the topsoil and preparing the seedbed, direct-sow flower seed only. The seed can have been collected locally (with the landowner's permission), or bought, or both. This method means that the flowers will not be in competition with grasses and, although at first there will be plenty of bare patches of ground – not in any case a bad thing for a butterfly meadow – during the second and third years these can be filled in either by sowing more seed or allowing self-seeding. This method enables you to sow a relatively large area with a relatively modest amount of seed.

There is one species of grass that grows so slowly that it may be sown along with the flower mixture, and this is sheep's fescue. The more vigorous red fescue or crested dog's-tail grasses should only be sown with the flower seed mixture if it is important to green up the site quickly, or if the site is exposed and erosion a problem. Crested dog's-tail produces a nice open sward but has little benefit for butterflies. Red fescues (there are number of different types) can quickly dominate the meadow, so sow very thinly. Make sure that you buy the wild seed and not the domesticated varieties.

You can also sow a cornfield annual mixture. This gives you colour in the first year. Then if you add two biennials, kidney vetch and viper's bugloss, they will give colour in the second year. By the third year most of the perennials will be flowering.

2. Sow locally-collected flower seed in seed trays (especially the plants that do not germinate well from sowing directly into the meadow area). When large enough, plant out into the meadow.

3. In year two or three of the meadow, sow hand-collected grass seed into the meadow. There needs to be fescue in the mix – red and sheep's – and common bent. These are fine grasses that are the foodplants of butterflies such as the Small Heath and the Marbled White. Another to collect in wild meadows is smooth meadow-grass, a favourite of the Meadow Brown.

After the grasses have begun to establish themselves in the meadow, sow yellow rattle. Yellow rattle is semi-parasitic on grasses and it is pointless to sow it until its host plants are present. It is an annual that germinates early in the year but only reaches maturity when its roots come into contact with the roots of grasses. Where it grows thickly it is noticeable how the surrounding grasses are stunted. This makes it a good tool in controlling grass. Do not sow it in areas of long grass, or it will soon be swamped.

A basic seed mix for the first year that would encourage butterflies and suit most soils might be:
• Grasses: sheep's fescue.
• Wildflowers: agrimony, bird's-foot trefoil, bladder campion, cowslip, devil's-bit scabious, field scabious (if site is well drained)), betony, cut-leaved and dove's-foot cranesbill (these will have to be hand collected), meadow vetchling, rough hawkbit, common (or lesser) knapweed, dyer's greenweed, ragged robin (gives a good early display), ox-eye daisy (this plant could dominate the meadow so sow sparingly), sorrel, kidney vetch, viper's bugloss, and cornfield annuals (common poppy, cornflower, corn cockle, corn marigold and corn chamomile).

There are many other species you could sow or plant which, though not as important for butterflies as these, will still provide some nectar: meadow buttercup is a good example.

Check against the chart at the end of the book to see which plants will suit your soil.

The best time to sow the seed is in September and October. Many – if not most – seeds germinate best if they have the winter cold to break down the their hard coats; this is, after all, when most seed falls to the ground naturally. I have had most success with seeds collected by hand and then sown immediately. Seed houses do a very good job when they collect, clean and store seed. But the seeds of some species seem to go into a dormant state with this treatment, and are then hard to germinate.

Some species germinate readily, however. Annuals, biennials and short-lived perennials are, as a very rough rule of thumb, in this category. They are the pioneer species, the ones that can dominate the meadow in the first years, especially in fertile meadows. Ox-eye daisy is a good example. It will dominate many meadows in the first years but, as the sward closes over, will gradually disappear. The exception to this is on banks where there is soil slippage and it can find fresh soil in which to germinate.

When sowing you can bulk the seed up with sand or sawdust. These light-coloured materials show up against the darker soils and let you see where you have sown, which helps give a better distribution. Rake the seeds gently into the soil; you do not want to bury small seeds.

Small Copper

This is the one species that any meadow-maker should be able to attract to their meadow. It is a widespread butterfly, colonial in nature but, like the Common Blue, colonising new habitat quite quickly. In the south there are usually three broods a year, and in warm years sometimes four. The early brood emerges in May and the females look for large sorrel plants growing in warm, long grass.

I cut paths through areas of my meadow in May. While cutting I am looking for sorrel, and the path I cut often includes some interesting curves to leave large sorrel plants to the north of it. These sorrels then grow into the warm, sheltered base of the path, ready for inspection by Small Copper females. The males will set up territories on these paths waiting for the females to come by.

The next brood emerges in July and the males are to be found in bare, dusty areas where they pugnaciously defend their territories. The females look for fresh growths of sorrel or sorrel seedlings. For this reason, small areas of the meadow could be cut in late June so that some re-growing sorrel is ready for the females at the right time. If your soil is acidic, sow sheep's sorrel next to paths. This is an annual and needs to grow in sparse grassland if its seeds are to stand a chance against taller growing plants. In some areas the Small Copper is present even though there is very little sorrel. These insects are probably laying on docks.

I find that the later broods spend a lot of their time nectaring and are particularly attracted to tansy and fleabane.

ABOVE AND LEFT *Small Copper.*

Chapter Six

The Long and the Short of it

Although I have been extolling the virtues of low-fertility meadows, there is also good reason, especially if you have a large garden, to consider cultivating an area of long grasses, where fertility will be higher. Although 'species poor' as far as plants are concerned, this part of the garden may be 'species rich' in invertebrates and small mammals.

Midsummer in the long grass meadow.

LEFT *Cocksfoot.*
ABOVE *Yorkshire fog.*

Two of the coarse grasses which may be grown here are especially important for the common golden skippers (Large, Small and Essex Skipper). Yorkshire fog and cocksfoot are tall grasses that like fertile soils. In the wild, grassland with these sorts of grasses tend to have low numbers of wildflowers: the skippers lay their eggs on the grasses but their nectar supply is poor. As a consequence, the skipper populations remain low. But if you arrange areas of fertile soils with tall grasses next to areas of low fertility rich in wildflowers, the numbers of these skippers go sky high. Should you have a meadow or rough bank of long wild grasses that you do not wish to disturb, you could indulge in a little topsoil stripping at one side and see if this affects numbers and species of butterflies.

Even though the golden skippers use these coarse grasses as their foodplants, they still like to lay in warm situations. Coarse grasses on the edges of paths are especially favoured. When designing your meadow you could consider making paths the dividing line between the areas of low fertility and high fertility.

MAKING MEADOWS IN EXISTING LAWNS

If you do not want to, or cannot get involved in, topsoil stripping can still make a valuable butterfly meadow. The habitat to consider here is scrub edge habitat, where long golden grass merges with the dark green of scrub or hedge.

Again, it is necessary to provide the things that butterflies like: sun and shelter, a good nectar supply and the right foodplants, and for most meadow butterflies, the right foodplants are grasses. I have described how to give wildflowers a head start in trying to achieve a balance between grasses and wildflowers, but not only do the majority of the commoner meadow butterflies lay their eggs on grasses, they are also generally the most numerous butterflies in the meadow. Grasses will eventually form a large proportion of the plants in a meadow, so it is important to emphasise that you must make sure they are the right grasses.

If you want to convert a lawn to a wildflower meadow, the simplest way is just to let it grow. You might be surprised at the species already present but unable to flower because of the cutting regime. How fertile is the ground? The height the grass grows to by early July will give you an idea. If it is almost up to your waist, the soil is highly fertile; below the knee, it is moderately fertile. Are there fine grasses? If the lawn has been regularly cut for many years, the grasses will be mostly fine to medium. The wildflowers that survive in a lawn are mostly low-growing, rosette-forming species such as daisies, self-heal and plantains.

There are three ways to introduce wildflowers to an area of grassland: one, by planting plug plants; two, by exposing the soil and sowing seed; three, by planting bulbs. All are easy to do but may not be successful. The common factor behind lack of success is competition from other plants. Small plug plants can have a high mortality rate in an established lawn or meadow, and the same is true for seedlings and bulbs trying to compete with tall grasses.

Plug plants can be bought from wildflower nurseries in large numbers, relatively cheaply. The best time to introduce them is in the autumn. First cut the grass very short, then take out a small area of grass and plant the plug in the exposed ground. This will mean the plant has the whole winter to settle in before there is too much competition. Make sure that you pick species that will suit the fertility of the meadow: it is all too easy to put in plants that will require an expedition to find by the following July.

Bulbs are easily introduced, and bluebells (but not the Spanish bluebell), daffodils and snake's-head fritillary are all worth trying.

If your meadow is fertile and damp there is a whole category of colourful, robust wildflowers capable of competing with the grasses. Some of these plants are particularly useful as they not only compete successfully but are also good nectar plants; some have another helpful feature – they spread by underground runners. Many plants of damp situations do not bother much with seed because it is so easy to send a root sideways through soft mud and then come up as another plant. However, many of these plants will also grow and reproduce in drier environments.

Although only large bird's-foot trefoil, listed in the panel on the left, is a butterfly food-plant, most are foodplants of moths. Wet and marshy grassland supports a large number of moth species but, unless you search for them, most will remain hidden.

There is one moth that makes a spectacular appearance. This is the Ghost Moth. Down in the damp hollow, just as dusk turns to night, a spectral dance is performed. Ghost Moth males, which are luminous white, gather to perform their pendulations. Just like a clock's pendulum, they rapidly swing back and forth. It has to be seen to be believed. The creamy white females, which gather at the lek to watch, will pick the moth which pendulates the best.

If your lawn is only moderately fertile then you could try all the typical meadow plants plus those in the panel, although I would favour the lower-growing species: common (lesser) knapweed*, field scabious*, cowslip, Devil's-bit scabious*, betony*, bird's-foot trefoil*, dyer's greenweed, agrimony, lady's bedstraw, musk mallow and spiny restharrow would be a good, colourful start.

Another method of introducing wildflowers into existing meadows is to first cut the grass short, then give the ground a good going over with a rake. You could even dig up patches of turf. The idea is to expose lots of bare ground and then sow wildflower seed into it. The best time to do this in the autumn. The plants that work best with this method are those that germinate easily: ox-eye daisy*, ragged robin*, yellow rattle and rough hawkbit*.

There are a number of species that germinate better if their seed is rubbed gently between two sheets of sandpaper before sowing; this helps to break down the hard outer

---

Plants that spread vegetively or by underground runner.

Those with an asterix are also very good butterfly nectar plants. Fleabane*, meadowsweet, meadow rue (this one lives up to its name and can dominate, but hoverflies love it), tansy*, valerian*, bistort (you can make the famous Easter ledges pie from this), watermint*, yellow flag, hemp agimony*, marsh woundwort, crosswort.

Robust plants that can cope with tall grasses but do not spread by underground runners.

Comfrey (can take over and is huge), meadow cranesbill, purple loosestrife*, yellow loosestrife, large bird's-foot trefoil*, greater burnet, marsh thistle*, fragrant agrimony.

All the above plants cope well with a damp fertile soil. In a well-drained fertile soil you could try:
Common (or lesser) knapweed*, greater knapweed*, field scabious*, tansy*, valerian*, yarrow*, meadow cranesbill, fragrant agrimony, chicory and wild carrot.

Most fertile soils lie somewhere in between; try all the plants and they will soon tell you what they like.

Meadow rue and others in a wet fertile meadow.

coat. Most of the legumes respond well to this treatment, for instance, bird's-foot trefoil*, tufted vetch and meadow vetchling.

Sowing into exposed soil is also the ideal way to introduce additional species of grasses to your meadow. Identifying grasses is not easy: the illustrations in books on grasses are quite often difficult to decipher. But it is possible to buy a wide range of already identified grass seeds. I would always recommend buying wild seed and not the agricultural varieties. It is generally easy, though, to collect as much as you need from roadside verges.

Bulbs give early colour. The two main wildflower bulbs are wild daffodil and bluebell*, but others, like crocus, snake's-head fritillary and wild tulip, could also be planted. These work particularly well in a garden situation.

THE MEADOW OF THE MANY SMALL PATHS

The first meadow I made is well over 20 years old now. It has changed gradually. Some plants wax and wane, others do well for a while, then disappear. There has been a gradual shift, though, from fine grasses and low-growing wildflowers to taller grasses and more robust wildflowers. It is still full of flowers – they are just large flowers. I suspect that this gradual greening-up happens to many meadows, especially if they are only cut once and that cut is late in the year. There is a tendency to cut late because you want to wait until flowers have set seed and caterpillars have found refuge. If this system of management results in a gradual deterioration of the habitat there has to be a different approach.

One way is to have a rotation system, whereby part of the meadow is cut twice in the year, and another area is cut twice the following year. Another way to get back to low-growing plants again is by stripping areas of turf. The third way is to create 'the meadow of the many small paths'. Do this by cutting lots of small paths through your meadow, initially with

Small paths meadow.

a strimmer or power-scythe. Remember to remove the cut material. Direct your paths through any coarse vegetation. The result is islands of wildflowers within a maze of paths. If you want to, you can even make a or labyrinth of it.

Once the course of the paths has been established, the paths can be kept short with an ordinary lawn-mower. At the end of the season the meadow is cut as normal and the following year a new system of paths is cut. This method has many advantages for the smaller meadow:

• The maze of paths lets you get to all parts of your meadow.
• The regular cutting of the sward will encourage finer grasses and smaller plants.
• Butterflies will like the small heat traps created between the wildflower islands.
• Foodplants growing in the paths, and to the side of the paths, will be particularly attractive to some butterflies. For instance, the second brood of the Small Copper will like the regenerating sorrel, the Common Blue will favour the fresh leaves of bird's-foot trefoil, and skippers will like the sun-blasted south side of Yorkshire fog and cocksfoot.
• If the paths are cut in a different pattern the following year then some of the finer plants will be gradually brought back to the whole meadow.
• Annuals are not forced out, as they will be if a large area is cut two or three times a year.

For the birds.

At Ryewater there are two fields sown with plants chosen to attract seed-eating birds in the autumn and winter. The main seeds sown are niger, millet, sunflower and lucern. Then it was found that niger was also a very good nectar plant, used by a wide range of butterflies visiting these fields.

Red Admiral on niger.

ABOVE *Small Skipper.*
BELOW *The Essex Skipper has inky black tips to its antennae.*
BOTTOM *Large Skiper female nectaring next to a Small Skipper.*

The Grass Feeders

The following skippers and browns all lay their eggs on grasses. They are colonial butterflies but most will colonise suitable new habitat quite quickly. Many of them are regarded as common within their normal range. Grassland habitats are widespread, so many gardens will be fairly close to colonies of these insects. In the best meadows some of these butterflies can emerge in huge numbers.

The Skippers (family *Hesperiidae*)

There are eight species of skipper to be found in Britain. Three of these are known as 'golden' skippers because of their colour. They lay their eggs on grasses, principally cocksfoot and Yorkshire fog. They are the Small, Essex and Large Skipper and they like similar types of habitat – sheltered, wild grassland where the grass has been left to grow tall, with an abundance of nectar flowers close by.

The Essex tends to like drier grassland than the Small Skipper, and the Large is said to prefer wetter and more wooded areas. All three, though, are often found in the same place. They are seldom found far from their breeding sites and colonies may be supported by quite small areas of rough grass. In recent years, the Essex seems to have used new road developments as corridors to spread along. This skipper over-winters as an egg and would probably do best in grassland cut rotationally, with just one third of the long grass area cut each year.

Except for the black, ink-like spots on the underside of the ends of the antennae, this insect appears identical to the Small Skipper and is often overlooked because of this. The Small Skipper's antennae tips are usually orange or brown but I have come across some that are grey-black, which might cause some confusion – the black on the Essex's antennae, however, is more a shiny black.

The Large Skipper emerges about mid-June and is typically seen just in ones and twos, in contrast with the Small Skipper, which can – when it emerges in July – be quite numerous on good sites. A week or so after the Small Skipper, the Essex emerges. Because all three butterflies can often be found in quite small areas of rough grassland they may be ones which will colonise your meadow and be attracted to stay in even modest meadow gardens.

The Browns (family *Satyridae*)

All the browns lay their eggs on grasses and, in the meadow, the commonest species will probably come from this group. Most of the brown butterflies are generally sedentary but, in warm summers, individuals will wander away from the colony and colonize new, suitable habitat.

The Meadow Brown has the distinction of being Britain's commonest butterfly. It is one of the few found regularly in the centre of large meadows: most others drift to the more sheltered edges. One of the favourite places for the female to lay her eggs is on long grass in a warm spot, conditions found next to a mown path. For this reason alone it is a good idea to cut a network of narrow paths through the main meadow.

Fescues, bents and meadow grasses are the main plants used for egg laying. Smooth meadow grass is thought to be one of its favourites. In my meadow, knapweed is much visited for nectar, then, when it has finished flowering, the hay field is deserted in favour of sunny banks, where marjoram and field scabious are still on the go. I suspect that we get a lot of butterfly refugees from neighbouring fields at this time, as these are mown or grazed long before ours and the butterflies come seeking uncut nectar plants.

The Ringlet emerges shortly after the Meadow Brown but prefers more humid conditions. It lays its eggs while flying or fluttering around, using a wide range of grasses. This butterfly will be found near the edges of the meadow where there is some shelter, and in damp grassland near trees and shrubs.

The Marbled White likes well-drained and sheltered grassland. Fescues are important for the first stage of its larvae; they move onto other grasses later. It is important, consequently, to maintain a range of grasses. Again, knapweeds, marjoram, scabious and thistles are favoured nectar plants.

The Marbled White has its strongest colonies in the south west of England. If you live in an area where it is common then make every effort to provide suitable habitat as it is a beautiful insect. It likes areas of medium to long grass. Huge numbers can build up on sunny banks that are minimally managed but dominated by red fescue.

The young larvae feed first on fescues, then progress to coarser grasses. Like the adult butterfly, it is very evident, as in good weather it is constantly on the move.

The Gatekeeper likes hot, sheltered positions, keeping close to hedgerows and scrub. This insect is a marjoram addict. It nectars on other flowers in ones or twos but covers the marjoram. After the Speckled Wood it is probably the easiest brown to create habitat for in the small garden. A south-facing hedgerow, long wild grasses growing below, mounds of marjoram nearby, and the Gatekeeper will be content.

Another of the grassland browns is the Small Heath. It is not as common as some butterfly books suggest: I am lucky to see any in my meadow. Places where I do find them, though, include old abandoned quarries where there are areas of fine grasses next to patches of bare ground. In some seaside areas, too, behind the dunes, they are bright flashes of orange, always on the move. They seem like a different species compared to the duller, more laid-back specimens I find in my meadow. This was a very common butterfly at one time but – like the Wall Brown, which likes similar habitat – it has declined over the last 20 years.

The Wall favours warm, dry grassland, preferably with bumps and mounds, bare ground and hollows. Chalk downs, coastal grasslands and quarries are the sorts of places this species favours. In warm years, however, numbers can increase dramatically and it may be found far from its usual haunts. Although the Wall is colonial, some individuals are great wanderers.

The Speckled Wood (see picture on page 36) likes mature gardens but it will also be attracted to the edges of your meadow, where there is scrub, hedgerow and dappled sunlight. It will also come down to nectar on flowers within the meadow.

In Scotland, an exquisite butterfly called the Scotch Argus is found. Its velvety, dark chocolate-brown wings have to be seen before you can appreciate what a gem of a butterfly this is. It is found in Dumfries and Galloway and large parts of the Highlands and comes into gardens within these areas to nectar. It is understandable why any urge to reproduce its habitat – miles of moorland and bog, already surrounding these gardens – might be resisted.

Top *Male Meadow Brown.*
Above *Female Meadow Brown.*

Below *Ringlet.*

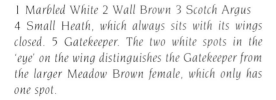

1 Marbled White 2 Wall Brown 3 Scotch Argus
4 Small Heath, which always sits with its wings
closed. 5 Gatekeeper. The two white spots in the
'eye' on the wing distinguishes the Gatekeeper from
the larger Meadow Brown female, which only has
one spot.

Very Low-Fertility Meadows

So far we have considered the creation of meadows which will chiefly attract wandering but-terflies and the commoner meadow butterflies. But, like fishermen who have enjoyed fishing for the local perch and bream, we now fancy a bit more of a challenge. A salmon? We need to bait our hook with something special. The rarer butterflies are sensitive creatures and in the next section we will be considering how to create habitat for some of them. They tend to like very warm spots where their foodplants grow. So, while we are stripping the topsoil, we could in some particular hot spots go one step further.

By stripping the soil down below the sub-soil to the next layer – usually loose rock or clay – we are lowering the fertility another degree. Plants in this sort of environment really struggle. Bare patches may still be quite apparent in the sward three or four years after sowing. After four years, the sward has usually closed but, even at the height of summer, it will only be seven to ten centimetres (three to four inches) high. These meadows are hot stuff for butter-flies. The photograph on the next page shows that even two years after sowing the plants are still tiny sprigs. But they continue to grow and by the fifth year they are a reasonable size. This very slow growth allows us to continue to sow seed for the first three years, and if you examine the photograph at the top of page 101, you will see just how many plants can be squeezed into a small area.

An attractive meadow of low-to-medium fertility soils, but, compared with the meadow pictured at the top of the next page, the sward is still quite high.

Mid-summer, and the sward does not reach the handle of my coffee mug. This photograph was taken seven years after the creation of the meadow. Although very low, all the bare patches in the sward have been filled in.

For those with a small garden this is a way of having a really intensive meadow. A word of caution though: keep these areas well separated from fertile areas. A path all the way round the stripped area would be a good barrier. And you may not want what could look like a patch of dried mud for two or three years in your garden. There are ways round this, however. One solution is to sow a lot of kidney vetch seed. As long as the patch does not have

Two years after sowing, and the plantlets are still tiny.

Five years after sowing. Note the high number of individual plants. The spotted leaves are Common Spotted Orchid.

water hanging around in pools over the winter, kidney vetch will appreciate the lack of competition and create a low sward. Another is to cover the stripped area with a thin layer of an attractive gravel. You could even make patterns with different colours. You then sow your seeds into the gravel. In addition, you could plant plug plants of creeping species such as germander speedwell, mouse-ear hawkweed, bugle, thyme and wild strawberry.

A gravel layer improves the appearance of bare soil.

The Dingy and the Grizzled Skippers

As an introduction to the rarer butterflies let us consider two skippers, the Dingy and the Grizzled, that are quite different to the golden skippers we have looked at so far. For a start, they do not lay their eggs on grasses. The Dingy's foodplant is generally bird's-foot trefoil. The Grizzled uses some small members of the rose family: its favourites are wild strawberry, agrimony and creeping cinquefoil. They both like sparse, sheltered grassland and are often found flying together. They are commonly found in abandoned quarries and on derelict industrial land – brownfield sites. When we strip topsoil we produce conditions similar to those in places like this – places where food-plants grow in short, sparse, sheltered grassland.

However, unless drainage is very rapid, these conditions in your meadow will only last for a few years before vegetation becomes too high and dense to be ideal. The Dingy Skipper, if it is found close by, may colonise your site for these few years. I have found the Grizzled to be less mobile than the Dingy. Most of the butterflies that are featured in this book have colonised one or more of the projects described; the Grizzled is one of the exceptions.

RIGHT *Dingy and* FAR RIGHT *Grizzled Skippers. One of the reasons why these two butterflies do so well on brownfield sites is that the lack of management means very little disturbance: no annual cut or grazing interrupts the development of egg, caterpillar or pupa. The fertility is so low that it takes many years for these sites to turn from grassland to scrub. When they do, the butterflies gradually disappear.*

The laying down of gravel introduces another technique of meadow-making, which is laying down substrates over a stripped area. A thin layer of gravel or other substrate (see Chapter 7) maintains the low fertility of the ground and is helpful in other ways.

• It creates a microclimate. Moisture is retained between the individual pieces of gravel and this aids germination.
• The top couple of centimetres of soil will be very well drained and many plants like this, as do many species of invertebrates. The technique is particularly useful on clay, where it can be difficult to create a seedbed.
• Substrates often contain lime, which allows you to grow a different range of plants.

The slow development of a site can have additional wildlife benefits – for instance, attracting specialist bees and wasps and other insects to burrow in the bare patches.

Bumps and Hollows

Exploiting low-fertility soils is a way of making meadows that, with a little patience, rewards you with an intricate tapestry of shapes and colours. With any fertility at all, small bumps and hollows, rocks and scree disappear under the vegetation. With this low-fertility method, any shapes that you make remain obvious, through to the end of the season.

This is true even with small pools. Dig a shallow hole, lay down pond liner or a couple of layers of damp-proof liner, and cover this with five to eight centimetres (two to three inches) of the dug material. The pool may dry up in the summer, but there is wildlife that thrives in this kind of environment. You could even have a series of pools, or a stream serviced by a water pump.

A 5cm (2in) layer of oolite was laid down over clay around the Gnome's House (see Chapter 8). The main flowering species seen here is bird's-foot trefoil.

Cornfield annuals are usually sown into prepared and fertile seedbeds and are often used to provide colour in the first year of the meadow. They can still be used in very low-fertility meadows; they just come out smaller, like a meadow made from Lilliputian. Sow in the autumn for best results.

Around the pools, low wetland plants can be grown that might get lost next to ponds of higher fertility. Marsh valerian, lady's smock, meadow thistle (this one is tricky, though), bugle and ragged robin are all good butterfly nectar plants in this situation.

After the topsoil has been removed, it is possible to create all manner of earthworks, using rocks, limestone dust, the subsoil itself or some other substrate on top of the subsoil – low fertility remaining key. On south-facing slopes you could make small ridges. To do this, lay out a line of rocks roughly east to west and fill in behind, on the north side, with a substrate of some kind, to create a terrace. Where the substrate is deepest, lower-growing flowers can be planted or sown; where the substrate is shallower, plants will grow higher, helping to create hot spots next to the rocks. Trailing plants like horseshoe vetch will grow over the rocks. And don't stop at ridges: you can make small bumps and mounds, undulations, gullies, or even cliffs. Shaping the land with earthworks like this is great fun. Obviously, the more 'natural' your landforms look, the better. Remember to consider how the sun will hit these shapes and, particularly if the materials are expensive, concentrate them in areas that get the sun for most of the day.

Pool with marsh valerian.

Making small mounds with oolite (see Chapter 7).

RIGHT *The same small mounds three years later. The tops of the mounds were planted with plugs of horse-shoe vetch, which soon covered them. Besides being a good nectar plant, it is wonderfully scented.*

Management

Most meadows will need cutting at the end of the season. Some newly created areas of very low fertility can often be left for two or three years before there is enough vegetation to warrant cutting. If the meadow is left uncut in areas of longer grasses, the dead vegetation tends to swamp the finer plants. After cutting, always remove the cut material; this helps to reduce the fertility of the meadow.

The best cutting tool for the small meadow is the strimmer. It is immensely versatile. With it you can cut steep banks, path edges, uneven ground and between trees. You can cut the vegetation to any height and choose to leave flowering plants uncut. Always wear safety equipment, especially goggles: small twigs and other bits of vegetation can be sent flying towards your face at an alarming velocity and could do serious damage to your eyes. A strimmer is noisy but fairly easy to use, and there is no reason to cut everything at once. I tend to spend all autumn cutting my meadow, doing a little at a time. I start in September, first cutting areas that are of less interest to butterflies, and gradually work through the rest of the meadow.

Larger areas are best cut with a power-scythe of some sort. The greatest problem, or the most tiring, is raking up all the cut material afterwards. However, if you do this work during a dry spell, it is much easier: there will be less dead weight of water to move.

If you have a large meadow you might be able to persuade your local farmer to cut it for hay. Unfortunately, he will probably want to mow in late June, as this is when the hay will have the most value to livestock. For the butterfly meadow this is too early. Some farmers will be happy to cut as late as August if they are given the hay, or you may need to pay him to cut and take away the hay at this time. Alternatively, you could suggest he puts cattle on to graze it all down in September.

You could also choose to keep livestock yourself and graze the land rotationally. Quite a

lot of ground, though, is needed even for one cow or horse, and it is never fair to keep just one of these animals. The old breeds of cattle are thought to be some of the best animals for grazing wildflower meadows. Wild breeds of horses like the Exmoor or the Shetland can be used, but horses tend to be patchy grazers. Water buffalo are used at Ryewater, and they are excellent grazers. Sheep are tricky as there always seems to be something going wrong with them; they also have to be sheared once a year. The Soay sheep – which is almost a wild breed – needs little attention and sheds its own fleece, but it is lightweight and you will need quite a few to keep the grass down. It is also good at escaping, so the meadow will need to be well fenced. Then there are llamas, alpacas and vicunas. These South American animals seem to be less trouble than a lot of other grazing animals, but they are quite expensive. Goats tend to be browsers and are better at knocking back areas of scrub. No matter which animal you choose, there will be problems and expense.

Water buffalo at Ryewater.

Part Three:
The
Specialist
Butterflies

Chapter Seven
The South Facing Bank

The Dragon Path at Ryewater.

'I know a bank where on the wild thyme grows'... and horseshoe vetch, rockrose and marjoram: it could be in your back garden. Many of the rarer butterflies are at the limits of their northern range in Britain. They are found in warm places where their foodplants grow in short or sparse grassland. Not being butterflies ourselves, we do not always perceive the striking range of temperature gradients that can occur down at ground level. Bare ground soaks up the sun and radiates the warmth back out; tall vegetation filters the sun's rays and keeps the ground level cool and moist.

The fertility of the soil affects the height and type of vegetation that grows in it. Moist, fertile soils produce a tall sward, whereas with thin soils the vegetation will be lower. If there is good drainage as well as thin soil, the environment for plants becomes even harsher. The low vegetation of thin, well-drained soils means that the ground is warmer and moisture evaporates quickly, helping to create still harsher conditions. Plants adapted to these stressful situations tend to have long taproots that can find moisture deep in the ground. In normal soils, they would be unable to compete, but in these conditions the taller plants, which would otherwise suffocate them, do not thrive. Many of these plants are of importance for butterflies, and one environment where they will flourish is the well-drained, south-facing bank.

Some of the best south-facing banks are found on chalk and limestone grasslands. These rocks are largely calcium carbonate. Chalk and oolite are soft rocks and can soak up moisture being almost 100 per cent calcium carbonate. Carboniferous limestones are much harder, contain less calcium carbonate, and water runs off them rapidly. The softer rocks produce landscapes rounded by weather (chalk downland is a good example of this) while the carboniferous rocks, being harder, do not weather so easily and produce rougher, craggy landscapes.

These rocks all produce soils rich in lime (calcium carbonate) and there are many plants that like limey (alkaline) soils. As we have seen, such plants are known as *calcicoles*. Plants that like acidic soils are known as *calcifuges*. Gardeners will be well aware of plants that like alkaline conditions and those that prefer acidic soils. The soils that are limiest are those where the rocks are closest to the surface – usually on slopes or near cliffs. In these areas, water run-off washes away the soil from the steep slopes, exposing the rock, which constantly refreshes the lime content of the soil. Where the soils are deeper, at the base or top of the hill, the lime is leached out; this soil then becomes more acidic and we get the strange mixture of *calcicoles* growing next to a *calcifuge* such as gorse.

Chalk and limestone hillsides are famed for their profusion of colourful flowers growing in short springy turf. The grasses – mostly red and sheep's fescue – are fine and hair- like. But such turf does not appear just because of the steep slopes. It has taken centuries of grazing to produce this mix of plants. Our task is to reproduce this habitat in our gardens.

Bank Construction

A science teacher called Jack Doyle experimented with one approach in the 1960s. He made a series of small mounds out of pure chalk in his back garden, then sowed and planted chalk-loving plants. It worked. I visited these mounds many years later and it was amazing to see these well-established mounds transforming a back garden into a miniature chalk landscape.

In the 1980s, when I was first exploring the stripping of topsoil, I began to wonder what would happen if we used the stripped top- and subsoil to create south-facing banks. We could cover the south-facing side with chalk or some other alkaline material. On the north-facing side of the bank we could grow shrubs and trees. It would provide a first class butterfly habitat. The area with stripped soil would become short, sheltered grassland. The bank, faced with a material such as chalk, would be suitable for growing a different range of plants and, because it is south-facing, bake in the sun. It would almost be like transporting your garden several kilometres south.

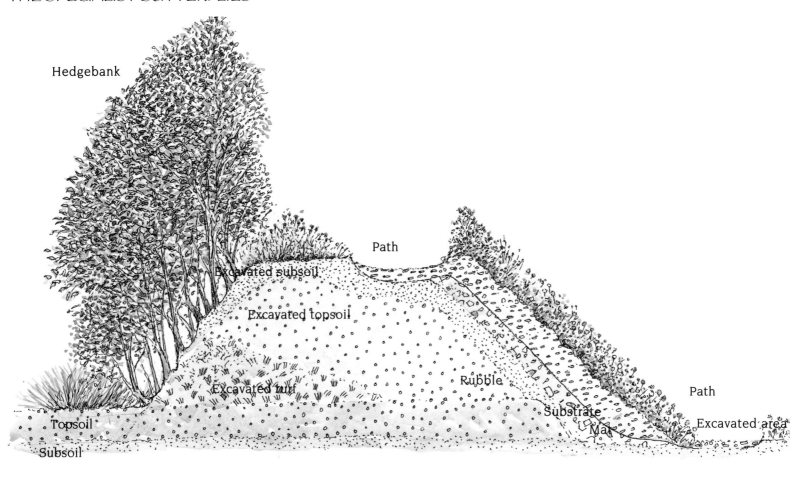

Hedgebank

Path

Excavated subsoil

Excavated topsoil

Excavated turf

Rubble

Path

Substrate Mat

Topsoil

Excavated area

Subsoil

Section through the first big mound.

Covering only the face of the bank with chalk, rather than using it to construct the whole thing, would mean much less material would be needed. On top of the bank there could be a path to enable you to explore the area, separating the south-facing bank from the richer soils of the north-facing side. The trees and shrubs to the north would not only help to create shelter but also provide another range of plants of benefit to butterflies.

This was my theory – and it worked too. The first mounds were small (particularly in comparison with some I have made since) but they allowed me to experiment. I was able to explore the idiosyncrasies of the plants I wanted to grow and iron out the problems.

STEP ONE

The size of the mound will depend on what space is available, but even in an area of three to four square metres you can make a respectable heap. Like creating a meadow, make sure that water has a way to escape, and beware of underground cables and pipes.

You can make the mound any shape you like, but probably the best shape for a small-to medium-sized mound is the crescent. Imagine an orange segment with the inner curve facing the south. A crescent works well because it will receive the sun all day, with the inside of the west point getting the early morning sun and the inside of the east point getting sun in the late afternoon.

Depending on size and access, you can either dig by hand or use a machine. Mark out the site (see drawing on the next page), strip the turf and begin to shape the back of the mound. Make sure that you strip the turf away from where the inner edge of the mound will be. It is important to keep the richer topsoil well away from the substrate.

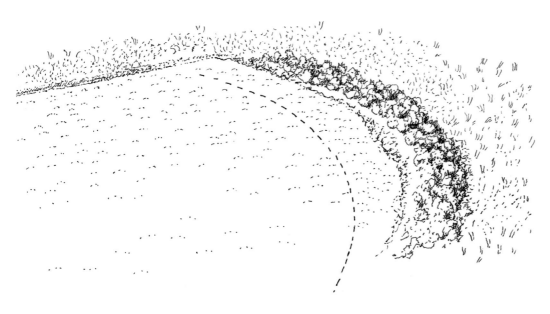

STEP TWO

Remove the next layer of soil and continue to shape the north side of the mound. Continue to keep the richer top soils as far as possible away from the top and south-facing sides. Then use a layer of subsoil to create the crescent shape. Small mounds will not be large enough to have a path running along the spine of the mound.

    The slope should not be steeper than 45°; any steeper and the bank could collapse. If you wish for a steeper profile you can hammer poles into the bank and use these as a support for wooden shelves that will hold up the substrate.

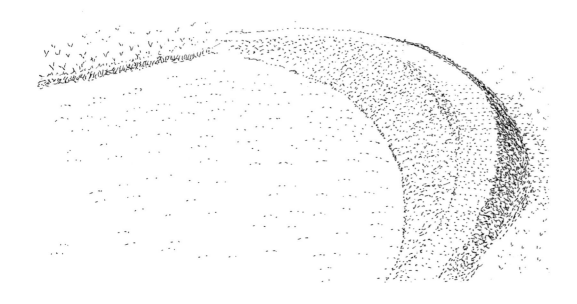

STEP THREE

We want to keep the substrate covering as far as possible away from the richer soils which have been used to shape the bank. This can be done by first putting down a layer of rubble (the best, but more expensive option) or a geotextile mat of some kind. Matting of various sorts is available from garden and building centres.

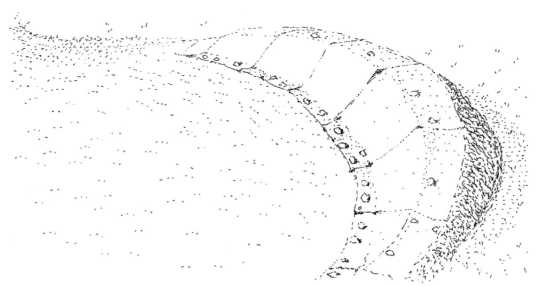

STEP FOUR

Now lay down the substrate. With a machine it is easy to drop it on and then shape it. By hand and wheelbarrow it could be poured from the top – it will slide down the mat. In either case, the substrate layer needs to be at least 15cm (6in) thick. It cannot be too thick but 30cm (1ft) should be more than adequate.

Which substrate to use? Chalk is ideal, even though not all of us live close enough to a source of chalk to warrant the cost of transport. I try to get my chalk when it is being extracted for housing developments or road widening schemes. With big projects this usually means that you buy it by the 10-, 16- or 20-ton truckload. Depending on distance, chalk can cost less than £10 per ton delivered.

Chalk is an excellent material but there will be some sort of substrate available wherever you live. In my own area, oolite is quarried. This is a soft rock which, when ground up, has many of the properties of chalk. Oolitic crusher-run, as the quarries call it, is a mixture of fine dust and rocks up to 12–15cm (5–6in) long. It is often used for making farm tracks. Portland and Doulting stones are very similar. Mendip dust – generally used for making mortar for building work – is also available in my area. It is ground-up carboniferous limestone. Some garden centres stock a wide range of gravels, stones and dust; this would be an expensive place to buy your material but useful for very small projects. When buying the stone, however, make sure that a proportion of the material is dust-like, otherwise moisture will drain out of the mound too quickly and all you will have is a pile of rocks.

It is also possible to construct a mound using waste of various kinds. One of my mounds was made from the sweepings of a stonemason's workshop floor. Other mounds have been made using rubble from a neighbour's demolished kitchen extension and outhouse. These were first constructed, then topped up with other substrates. In this way unsightly bits of breezeblock can be battered down and hidden.

Crushed concrete has a very high alkaline content and in one of my projects I used it neat, although there were probably other materials – such as brick dust – in the mixture. Any sort of ground-up stone material can be used, in fact, and it is fun to experiment.

To estimate the quantity of substrate you will need, I usually reckon that 10 tons will cover an area of 10–20m^2, depending on how thickly you lay it. If you are buying in smaller amounts, a small truckload of 5 tons or so will enable you to make a very respectable mound.

You will have to think about moving the material once it has been delivered. For large projects, a dumper truck will probably be necessary. However, most projects will be far smaller, and this is where the wheelbarrow and some strong backs are needed. Some substrates are easy to shovel into a wheelbarrow but others may solidify and need a pickaxe to break them up.

If the pile of substrate can be stored in the front garden, you could spend a few months slowly building the mound. By finding a source of local rocks, stone or gravel, mountain features can be incorporated such as gullies, screes, rock strata, ledges, cliffs, miniature standing stones, even glacial erratics. Study natural rock features to get ideas. Remember, though, that if these features are too small they may disappear from sight when the vegetation begins to grow. Different underlying rocks can mean there will be different drainage conditions, allowing you to grow a wider range of plants. Some plants like to grow between cracks; others prefer to be in full sun while their roots get a cool run behind a large rock. Thymes like to creep across the tops of bare rock, where there is little competition from other plants. This is also a good spot to grow some foodplants, such as horseshoe vetch and rockrose. As the plant bakes on top of the rock its roots are tucked in behind. You can see this at many cliff sites: the plants growing at the very edge of the cliff are often the most interesting. Here soils are shallow, there is more lime available, and the drainage is sharp.

If the mound is large enough to have a path across its crest then it is a good idea to cover the richer soils of the path with a mat as well, and then cover that with a thinner layer of substrate or subsoil. This helps prevent unwanted plants from the richer soils creeping up from the path to the bank.

Now is the time to plant and sow. There are hundreds of plants that could be grown in

RIGHT *Four years later.*

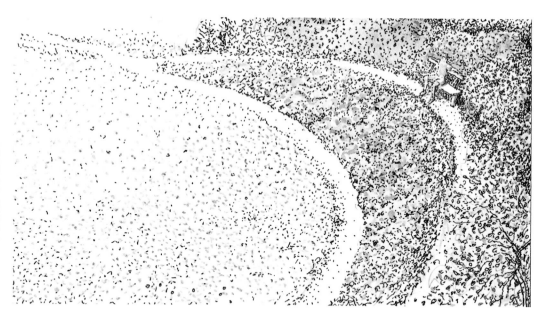

1 *The topsoil has been excavated and a layer of sub-soil is being laid on top.*
2 *To ensure the meadow area below the mound is completely infertile, a layer of clay is being excavated.*
3 *A geotextile mat has been laid down and covered in oolite.*

the bank but for butterflies there is a basic list. Plants that grow easily from seed should be sown; others may be better introduced as plugs or cuttings. You could try both methods.

SEEDING AND PLANTING

The Bank
Grasses
I would only sow wild sheep's fescue and, for ornamental effect, quaking grass. Other grasses will find their way in and may be unwanted. It is best to weed out all but the finer grasses.
Nectar plants (some of which are also foodplants)
Sow marjoram, greater knapweed and viper's bugloss. Plant plugs of thyme and small, field and Devil's-bit scabious. If the mound is small, grow all these plants (except the thyme) near the top: some are quite tall and we do not want them casting a shadow over the bank. Even on larger banks it is a good idea to concentrate the nectar plants next to the path at the top: the butterflies will be drawn there and it will be easy to observe them.
Foodplants (some of which are also amongst the best nectar plants)
These need to be in full sun. Sow kidney vetch, small amounts of bird's-foot trefoil and, if you can find it, seeds of cut-leaved cranesbill. Plant plugs or cuttings of horseshoe vetch, rockrose, wild strawberry and agrimony. Hairy violet and cowslip are both better in moist situations, peeping out from other vegetation.

Other plants that are of less value to butterflies but are used by other insects – or are highly colourful or in some other way interesting – are: dropwort, herb Robert, bloody cranesbill, purging flax, wild basil, germander speedwell (a striking colour contrast to grow among horseshoe vetch), wild candytuft (an annual that will die out unless you keep sowing it), bladder campion, nodding catchfly (grows better if a bit of clay is added around its feet), lady's bedstraw, tower mustard, mignonette, vervain, spiked speedwell, wild clary, meadow clary (the slugs always eat mine), clustered bellflower (difficult), nettle-leaved bellflower, harebell (I cannot get it to grow), teasel, crown vetch, woolly thistle and dark mullein (the last four only for large banks). Remember, you are creating a habitat but not guaranteeing the appearance of rare butterflies. However, all the commoner species will love the bank.

The same bank, two years after sowing and planting. Kidney vetch is providing most of the colour.

The Hedgebank or Shelterbelt

In a garden situation, ornamental shrubs such as buddleia and escallonia can be grown. In a wilder setting, buckthorn, privet, wych elm, holly, hops, honeysuckle, gorse, broom and ivy are more appropriate. And why not try barberry? The Barberry Carpet is one of Britain's rarest moths.

The Meadow

Treat the stripped area at the base of the mound as you would the low-fertility meadows of Chapter 5 and Chapter 6.

Nodding catchfly.

Make a lip out of the substrate to create a well-drained mound, on top of the existing mound.

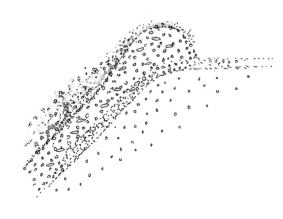

Everyone Is Different

One of the exciting things about constructing these mounds is that each one is different. In the wild, a plant will grow in profusion in some areas and not in others – though the areas may look similar to our eyes. Some plants have very particular requirements. Subtle differences in moisture availability, drainage, depth of substrate and aspect can all cause variations in the plant compositions of the mounds, even if they are made with the same substrates. In general, though, the deeper the free-draining material, the longer the bank will take to develop. This is because there will be less moisture available, and plants will be stressed. These banks are often the best in the long run but can be sparse for a few years.

Banks can even be made with a lip on the top (see drawing) to accentuate the free-draining nature of some substrates.

Some plants will grow in all the different substrates quite happily; others can be quite contrary. Horseshoe vetch, for instance, grows well on some mounds at first but then slowly dies back. Rockrose does not like growing in pure chalk; it is far happier in oolite, or even chalk mixed with clay. Wild strawberry will cover oolitic and crushed concrete but is slower to cover chalk.

I tried to grow nodding catchfly in oolite but it just died. Then I noticed it on cliffs along the south coast. It was growing in clay subsoil below a stratum of chalk. I reasoned that it must be receiving a downwash of chalky water, and set out to reproduce the same conditions on my bank. It worked. These sorts of experiments make mound gardening particularly exciting.

When making the mound you could use a few different substrates. On one mound I created a sea serpent, with a head and neck covered with crushed concrete, a body and flipper of chalk and a tail of oolite. You could also vary the depth of the substrates.

A clay bank made after excavations at the back of the house.

Clay Mounds and Banks

Many plants favour mounds; they like the extra drainage. The soil in a mound becomes crumbly and ants love making their nests in them. In short, just by shaping the ordinary soil in your garden into little hillocks, you can create wonderful bumpy meadows, allowing you to grow plants that might otherwise struggle.

The same principles apply as in the making of limestone mounds. An area that has had its topsoil taken away will, in only two or three years, look like ancient meadow. Mounds made with topsoil remain fertile so cover them with an infertile material. This time it should be clay or another subsoil. Having removed topsoil and created the mounds, you now take off the next layer – the subsoil or clay – and cover the mounds with it. You can introduce rocks into the mounds, if you like, or even small amounts of limestone. These mounds resemble the limestone mounds but are made with materials from the meadow itself.

With a machine mounding the topsoil and then covering it with a thick layer of clay or subsoil you can make wonderful banks. If you are ever having an extension put on the back of your house, you could use all the subsoil that is dug out for the foundations, and any rubble that comes with the work, to make new mounds.

The plants to grow on these banks include many of the normal meadow plants, but species more associated with limestone may also grow well, due to the improved drainage. Try marjoram and field scabious.

WEST-FACING BANKS

In the late afternoon many butterflies will gravitate towards the warmest part of the meadow, and a west-facing bank covered in plants rich in nectar will be a great draw. We do not need to be as concerned about foodplants so low fertility is less critical. This bank could be on the side of one of the south-facing banks. Grow all those taller nectar plants like hemp agrimony, teasel, field and Devil's-bit scabious, tansy, valerian, marsh thistle, and even bramble.

Mound Management.

The mound needs to be managed by cutting back its vegetation each year. Smallish mounds can be cut with hedge clippers. It is a bit like giving a crew cut. On very large banks a strimmer will have to be used. Remove all the cuttings.

To mimic downland grazing, small parts of the mound could be cut back in June to allow young, bushy regrowths of bird's-foot trefoil, horseshoe vetch and rockrose to attract some of the blues in July and August. Leave the cuttings where they are for a few days to let any caterpillars crawl off.

The path on the mound's crest will need to be mown a few times a year, and the hedge bank cut back to stop it spreading over the path. Weed out large clumps of coarse grass and any other plants you do not want.

Butterfly Mound Dramas

The crescent mound is like an amphitheatre, the actors are gathering. Down below a Common Blue male is perched on a stalk of grass, waiting for a female to mince by, but instead another male is seen and they both rocket skyward, tumbling in loop the loops – a blur of movement. They lose sight of each other and then descend to their original stalks of grass. Then they are up again: this time it is a Small Copper male that has caused the disturbance, and later a Small Blue. Sometimes all three species take to the air in a maelstrom. Three large Skipper males are doing their own version of this aerial dance. Once I was lucky enough to see male Green Hairstreaks behaving in the same way, but their launch pads were from prominent bushes.

Meanwhile, already-mated females of all these species are sneaking from foodplant to foodplant on the crescent, laying their eggs.

Later in the year, on the mounds of marjoram, lazy Gatekeepers are stuffing themselves with nectar, along with Meadow Browns and Marbled Whites, while below, second brood Small coppers and Common Blues are playing the chasing game. The mound is alive with movement – every flower head is twitching with butterflies, moths, bees and hoverflies.

Then, at the end of the butterfly season, it is the turn of the Small Tortoiseshells to feast on small scabious. All the hard work seems worthwhile.

Common Blue male and bloody cranesbill. In my own meadow, I find the area in front of the crescent mound is a favourite place for the males of a number of species of butterfly to perch and wait. The hard work has been done, the mound is made and a few years old, the sun is out and you can sit and watch the drama unfold.

Kidney vetch bank

Small Blue and kidney vetch

Despite being Britain's smallest butterfly, the Small Blue has a big presence. When seen in any number – fluttering scraps of baby blue – they fill the meadow with movement. This is a rare butterfly, yet it is possible to create habitat for it in an area the size of a large living room. It seems to be one of the most sedentary of butterflies, rarely moving beyond the sheltered nooks it likes.

The foodplant of the Small Blue is the of kidney vetch. This vetch is found in chalk and limestone grassland, dunes, quarries and railway cuttings. It tends to like south-facing banks with crumbly soils and grows in just the sort of dips and slopes that the Small Blue also favours.

The males emerge in mid-May, lingering at the base of banks, waiting for females to pass by. Once mated, the female searches for prominent kidney vetch flower heads. An egg, laid on the flower bud, hatches after a couple of weeks and the caterpillar burrows into the flower head. When it is larger it sits openly on the seed head, looking not unlike a seed head itself. In late July, the caterpillar climbs down to find a place under moss or in crevices in the ground. It lies dormant there until the following April, when it pupates.

A Small Blue colony has an astonishing ability to appear, year after year, on tiny parcels of land. On some sites only a handful of kidney vetch plants flower, but the colony persists. This may be because the caterpillar is so well hidden from predators – first on top of a kidney vetch plant and then in crevices in the soil – that the colony always manages to produce at least a few adults. Small Blues also tend to be found in

Mating pair of Small Blues.

THE SPECIALIST BUTTERFLIES

Small Blue laying eggs.

The Ogre's Chair mound with visiting children. Clive Farrell leads the party of school children around Ryewater. This mound was colonised within two weeks of the first kidney vetch flowering.

habitats that are almost self-regulating, like abandoned quarries. One of the greatest dangers to the caterpillar, in fact, is another Small Blue: they are cannibalistic if they find themselves on the same flower head.

The adult only lives one to two weeks and sticks very closely to its fragment of habitat. Yet, especially in really hot spells at the end of May to the beginning of June, some mated females will venture out to colonise new sites. In many areas of the countryside, kidney vetch is found only in tiny patches. Can you imagine setting out to find one of only, say, 10 parcels of land where kidney vetch grows – each just the size of a living room – in a vast kidney vetch-empty landscape? You have a week to do it, but can only travel when the sun is shining. This is the challenge for of the Small Blue. Add the fact that most Small Blue colonies are small and only a few, if any, females leave the colony, the chance of new habitat being colonised appears remote. Yet it happens. My own meadow was colonised and now has the largest colony of Small Blues in Somerset. Four other areas which I have created have also been colonised, one of them having the next nearest known colony some 20km (12ml) away. My own theory is that the Small Blue female can detect kidney vetch, especially where it grows in profusion, across very appreciable distances.

Mounds made within 500m (550yd) of an existing colony have been colonised in the first year the new kidney vetch flowered or, to put it another way, within two weeks of it being possible for the Small Blue to colonise these mounds, they have done so.

The mounds described in this section are ideal for the Small Blue. The sunnier and more sheltered the site, the more the Small Blue will like it. Kidney vetch, bird's-foot trefoil and horseshoe vetch make excellent nectar sources for the adults. They also need long grass to roost on.

If there were as many butterfly mounds as there are ponds in Britain' gardens, the Small Blue would become as common as the frog. Indeed, the butterfly mound is like an upside-down pond, and they could both be made together if the soil dug out for the pond is used to form the basis of the mound. These two habitat projects, the pond and the mound, bring more exciting wildlife to a small or medium-sized garden than any other.

There are two problems to overcome. Kidney vetch, although often described as a short-lived perennial, is, in effect, a biennial. It needs to find bare or crumbly ground each year for its seeds to germinate. What happens with many projects is that the plant does well for the first few years, then other plants gradually begin to fill available spaces, and the kidney vetch population diminishes until it is gone. This is why in the wild it does best on steep slopes, where soil is constantly being exposed. To counter this difficulty, collect some seed every year and make sure it is pressed down into newly-scraped areas. As it is a biennial, you will also have to remember to sow seed in the second as well as the first year of the bank or meadow. Otherwise it will, at least initially, only flower every second year.

The other problem is rabbits. They will eat the flower heads mercilessly – and no flower heads mean no Small Blues. If you find yourself with a 'gap year', when you know there will be no seed for the following year, do not panic. You can always buy plugs.

Mounds in the Liebert Garden

Tony Liebert has been a mound-maker for many years. When Tony and Annie Liebert bought their property, one of the first ventures they tried was growing wildflowers for sale. They built a series of low mounds simply by stripping off turf and piling it up. Tall wildflowers which like well-drained positions, such as knapweeds and scabious, were planted in the mounds and grew well.

Unfortunately, not many of the wildflowers sold. The mounds, however, prospered and attracted many butterflies. It was a short leap from making turf mounds to making limestone mounds. Tony ordered a lorry load of lime waste – what is left after the lime has been extracted from the rocks – and set about making his mounds. They are shaped to face south, and planted up with all the usual *calcicoles*.

In late July the mounds are like cakes, with an icing of marjoram, lady's bedstraw, knapweeds and scabious above a tablecloth of wild grasses. The butterflies mob the mounds like kids at a party. Some of the 'cakes' are beginning to melt. The wildflowers are leaking into the surrounding meadow and onto mounds made by Tony's secret army of mound-makers:

Meadowscape. After a time, the mounds blend into the landscape.

ants. The well-drained soil is ideal for these insects and the mounds they make are suited to many of the wildflowers we want to encourage.

Maybe it is because the ground has been relatively undisturbed for a long time that the ants find the conditions so attractive: mounds grow like giant mushrooms up and down the meadow. Whatever the reason, the different mounds allow him to experiment. After spotting heath (or common) speedwell on mounds in the Quantocks, he planted some on a mound in his meadow, and it is now covered with the plant. Other ant mounds have tiles placed on them for other invertebrates and reptiles to bask on or hide under.

The mound-making experiments continue, the latest being a lime 'bath', with the sides of the bath made from calciferous clay and the bath filled with lime sweepings, scalpings and fines. Gullies very much like the basins in the Bramblearium (see Chapter 8) have also been made, and small patches of heath.

The heath is created very simply by stripping off the topsoil and then planting up with heaths, heathers and gorse. Tony has well-drained, slightly acidic soil, in which heathers do well. At Ryewater, as an experiment, we made a small area of heath by importing 'overburden' sand. This sand has a lot of impurities in it and is not valued by quarries. It was laid over an area which had been stripped of its topsoil. The sand was then planted up with cross-leaved heath. All the plants are doing well, but others have not been added yet. Heath has the benefit of allowing you to grow a wide range of heathers, most of which are excellent nectar plants. It is worth remembering that the soils of prospective heaths need to be well drained, acidic and sandy.

Created heath with breeding nets in background.

Chapter Eight
The Wurm

W'hisht lads had yer gobs
A'll tell yees all an awful story
W'hisht lads had yer gobs
A'll tell yees about the wurm

All over the British Isles, and indeed other parts of the world, there are earthworks to be found: barrows, henges, dykes, tumps and burial mounds. Then there are standing stones, stone circles and stone rows. The purpose of many of these constructions is

An aerial view of the Wurm.

unknown but there are numerous theories, ranging from the sensible to the weirdly strange. I believe I know one of the reasons they were built: they just look good. When you come across a standing stone on a lonely moor, its vertical presence is very powerful. Earthworks, too, are imbued with drama and suspense. What might be inside?

Many of these earthworks attract butterflies too, their steep sides having protected them from 'improvement' and the plough. The construction of some of these sites took large numbers of people many years to complete but now, with the help of mechanical diggers, we can move large quantities of earth in an almost inappropriately short time.

If you are going to create a mound, why not give it a meaning other than its direct purpose of attracting butterflies? The following describes some meadows designed primarily for butterflies but with a story or idea attached. All the projects at Ryewater were also designed with young children in mind.

The Gnome's House at Ryewater. This unique house is covered in a damp-proof liner, then a layer of clay and oolite. The conditions on the roof are quite harsh, but conducive to the growing of many of the plants discussed in Chapter 7. To emulate this for a garden shed, ensure the shed is extremely sturdy in order to carry the weight of a butterfly meadow roof.

ABOVE Clouded Yellow laying on bird's-foot trefoil. The base of the Bramblearium is now covered in bird's-foot trefoil (see picture on page 103). Clouded Yellows are found here throughout the summer.
RIGHT One of the brambles next to a chalk bank.
BELOW The gnome, made by Rachel Hooten, looks out across Ryewater. Perhaps he is contemplating a breakfast of blackberries.

THE BRAMBLEARIUM.

At the end of the Bramblearium, on a high mound, lives the gnome in the gnome house. The gnome looks after the brambles. To complicate the story, he once was the ogre in the Sleeping Dragon story (see next example). As an ogre he ate too many pixies and all the blackberries, so he was condemned by the Master to eat blackberries, and nothing but blackberries. At the same time, he was turned from an ogre into a gnome. He looks after the brambles assiduously because he has nothing else to eat. He has collected many different sorts to give a little variety to his diet.

This Ryewater site was an ordinary agricultural field. The brief was to design a meadow for brambles. There are over 350 micro-species of bramble in the British Isles. Brambles are among the best nectar plants and this was excuse enough to create a meadow for them.

We created the meadow by making a series of five pudding-bowl shapes (see aerial picture page 52) in a narrow, 0.8ha (2ac) field. The topsoil was scraped off mechanically and piled around each bowl rim to make it higher. This created shelter and a suntrap on the floors and south-facing aspects of the mounds. Chalk was then laid down on each south-facing side, and planted up with all the species talked about in Chapter 7. On the floor of the bowls, a thin layer of oolite (see page 101) countered the wet clay surface, making it suitable for kidney vetch. Other plants were also sown, but especially bird's-foot trefoil. The base of the bowl has a Mediterranean feel, with lots of bare ground and bright plants dotted around.

The construction of the meadow was finished in 2000 and now, besides all the common meadow butterflies, it has colonies of Dingy Skipper, Green Hairstreak, Small Blue and Chalkhill Blue – there may even be Adonis. Marsh Fritillary has a toehold: it is seen in the meadow each year, and laid eggs once. Clouded Yellows are seen throughout the summer and, although these are wandering butterflies, seem to form annual summer colonies. They may even be managing to over-winter here in mild years.

THE SLEEPING DRAGON

Snakes, dragons, sea serpents and wurms all lend themselves to mound-making and there are all sorts of Celtic and Chinese myths that you can weave into stories to explain them. Earth energy is conducted down dragon paths, dragons guarding hoards of gold… But more practically, because of their sinuous bodies, you can twist them into the shapes that you want. The south-facing bay is the best shape to create suntraps, and serpents necks. bodies and tails can be curved to create bays .

One of the main purposes of mound-making is to remove topsoil and, in the poor sub-soil, create suitable conditions for a rich, flowering meadow. The topsoil is hidden inside the mound. A snakey shape can be stretched to many parts of the site and this means the topsoil does not have to be transported very far. One thing a driver of a digger dislikes is moving backwards and forwards with soil in his bucket. He wants to put it straight into a dumper truck or onto the final resting place. With a design of this sort, the digger can remove soil 30 feet away from the mound's course, turn and deposit the soil, and then turn round for the next scoop, all without moving from the spot.

This example, the Sleeping Dragon, has been made in a 16-acre field (see aerial picture on page 52) and large parts of the mound were made without much transporting soil from one area to another. Because of the size of the project it would have been too expensive to cover the mound with any material so, being rich topsoil, the grass on the mound has to be cut often. All north-facing banks are slowly being covered by gorse. The areas where the soil has been removed are now exciting meadows, rich with flowers.

LEFT *Plan for the Sleeping Dragon.*
BELOW *The Sleeping Dragon is a maze; there is only one true path to the Dragon Stone and it is not the straight and narrow one (see picture on page* 110).

THE DRAGON STONE

The master of Ryewater hid his treasure under a standing stone (the Dragon Stone), but he was seen burying the treasure by an ogre. He had to find a way of guarding the stone. He went to a second-hand dragon dealer to buy a dragon to watch over the stone. The dragon he bought was huge and the dealer told him it had only had one previous owner. The dragon wrapped his tail around the stone and promptly went to sleep. As everyone knows, when dragons sleep, they sleep for a very long time. This one has been asleep ever since.

Although the size of this project is huge, all its principles can be applied to small gardens. Many colourful wildflowers that can struggle in ordinary soils may find a home, if that soil is shaped or moved in some way. The stripped areas of the Sleeping Dragon (see page 68) now harbour a wide range of colourful wildflowers, and the mounded topsoil, especially on south-facing slopes of the Dragon, is slowly being colonised by many of the same flowers. The improved drainage is the main reason why plants fare well on the mounds, but there is also some mixing of sub-soils and topsoils. This suggests another technique, which is to bring subsoils to the surface and bury the topsoil – in other words, invert the soil profile to lower its fertility. The R-Field was made like this (see page 53). A chisel plough was used to invert the soils. The same can be done in a garden with a mini-digger or a spade.

The great spiral of the Sleeping Dragon.

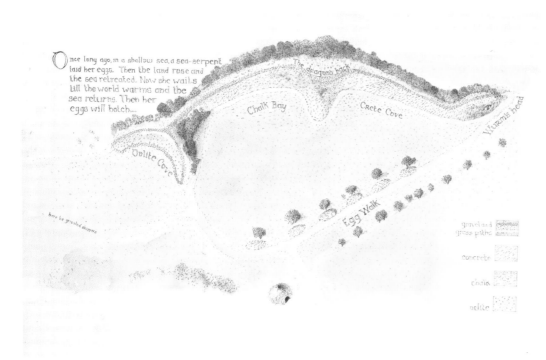

THE SEA SERPENT

A sea serpent laid her eggs in a shallow sea but before they could hatch the sea receded. She is waiting for the seas to rise (because of global warming caused by all the waste we produce?) and then her eggs will hatch.

This mound is on a landfill site. Carymoor Environmental Centre invited me to design a mound for butterflies on behalf of the West Country Branch of Butterfly Conservation. In fact, it is a mound on top of a mound. Underneath is layer upon layer of rubbish, capped with a metre-thick layer of clay. The butterfly mound on top of the rubbish mound is made in the shape of a giant sea serpent. To fit in with the idea of recycling, waste materials were used as much as possible.

The Sea Serpent is really three south-facing bays, with the head, neck and one half of a flipper forming one bay, the body and the other half of the flipper the second, and the tail the third. The first bay has been covered with crushed concrete. The second has been covered first with a layer of rubble and then with chalk waste from a building site. The third – and smallest – is covered first with a layer of rubble and then with oolite. The north-facing bank has been planted with a wide range of native trees and shrubs. There are also six small egg-shaped chalk mounds to the south of the Serpent.

There are differences in the plant compositions in the three different sections, with the crushed concrete performing reasonably well in comparison with the other two. After six years, some parts of the Serpent have got to the stage where they would benefit from a second cut, as some of the taller perennials are taking over. This cut could be done rotationally, with each area only cut twice in one year every three years. However, the Small Blue has now colonised the Serpent. This creates a problem. Cutting the bank twice a year would eventually remove the kidney vetch from the cut areas. But the kidney vetch would disappear anyway if the vegetation is allowed to remain tall. A compromise will have to be found, with areas with the least kidney vetch cut twice a year and reseeded from nearby sections.

THE WURM

The earth's energy travels down the Wurm to its tail, which spirals around the Bullaun. The Bullaun is a large rock. Depressions have been formed in the rock's upper surface. In each depression sits a large, medium or small stone. Those with a strong will can walk down the length of the Wurm. When you reach the Bullaun the power in the stone will be at its height. Then you have a choice. Turn a stone three times sunwise and you can make a wish or a blessing. Turn a stone three times widdershins and you can make a curse!

The Wurm was made on the floor of a small valley (see picture on page 126). While the banks of the surrounding small hills are rich in flowers, the base of the valley had a thick layer of top-soil. This area had to be cut two or three times a year to keep it tidy

As with the other mounds, the rich topsoil was used to make the Wurm and the south facing side has been covered with chalk. Most of the turf has been hidden in the base of the large spiral tail mound. Because the hillsides are covered in wildflowers, much of the seed needed for the project was collected by hand. It is useful to be able to recognise wildflowers at all their different stages, from seedling to seed head, and one of the best ways to gain this ability is to grow the plant yourself (see Chapter 10).

ABOVE *The Bullaun carved by Steve Bushell.*
BELOW *The chalk banks of the Wurm.*

THE HOP GARDEN
This small chalk bank (in construction) is backed by a trellis of fence posts and wire. Hop and honeysuckle will grow on the trellis. At one time hops were the favoured foodplant of the Comma and huge numbers of caterpillars were found on hops being grown for the brewing industry – hence the Comma carving.

133

THE SPIRAL

The brief here was to create habitat for the Small Blue and Chalkhill Blue, as well as other butterflies, without causing too much disturbance to an existing meadow. The meadow, part of a very large garden, slopes to the north, so a means of reversing the slope had to be found. A small sunken path provided the inspiration: a spiral trench could be dug. This would provide lots of south-facing slopes and, when the meadow was flowering, it would hardly be visible.

The initial task was to mark out the spiral. First, the spiral centre had to be found. The original drawing, done to scale, showed roughly where it should be. A fence post was hammered into the ground (see drawing on next page). Then a circle was marked out, with the fence post as the centre of the circle. The circle's circumference was then divided into eight, and each spot marked with a post. A length of string was tied to the central post and stretched to the spot where the spiral was to start. The string holder then walked in an ever-decreasing circle, as the string wrapped round the circle of fence posts. By a process of trial and error, by making the circle of fence posts larger or smaller, you get the spiral to start and end where you want.

This design gives a different dimension to a meadow, creating a subterranean walk that not only provides habitat for butterflies but also has a feeling of labyrinth as you spiral contemplatively to the centre…

When viewed from ground level, the spiral will be hidden by the flowering meadow.

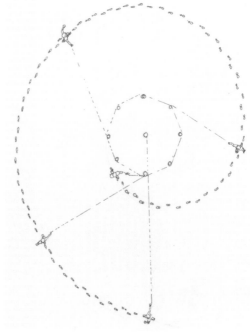

ABOVE How to mark out a spiral.

ABOVE LEFT This kind of project could only be considered well-drained soils. In damper soils all you would create is a very long pond. If your ground is well-drained and level, there is huge potential to turn it into an area full of south-facing slopes.

LEFT A few years later – a spiral of butterfly plants.

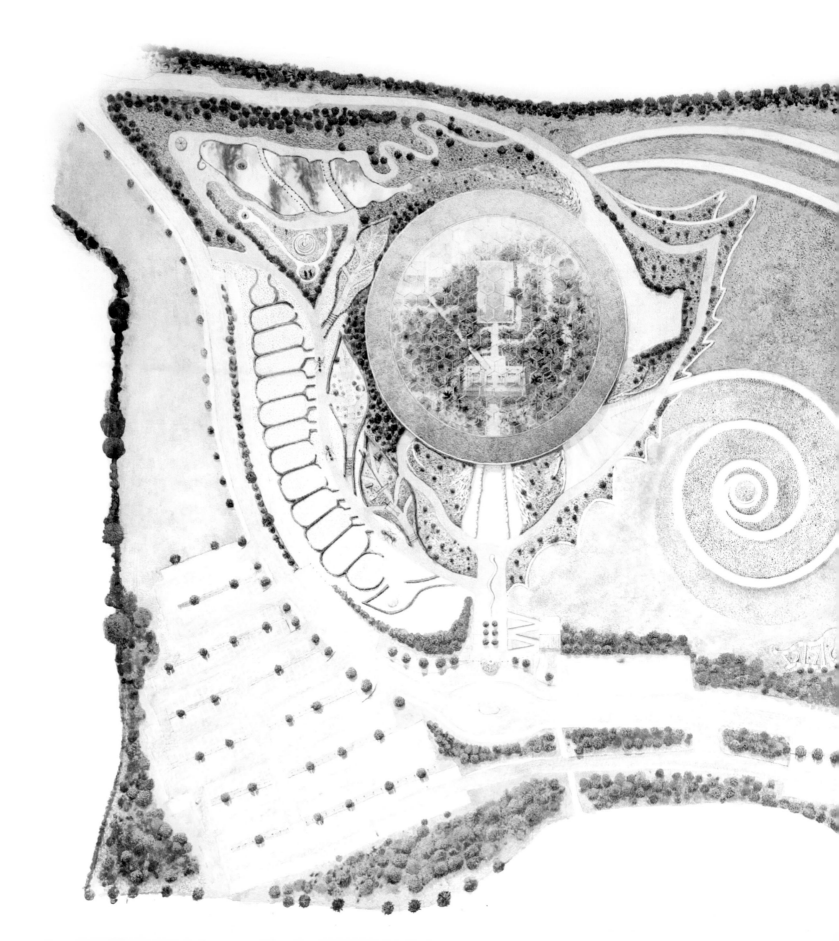

BUTTERFLY WORLD

This huge, ambitious project of Clive Farrell's is proposed for a site near St. Albans, just off the M25. Its design is based on the shape of a butterfly.

A tropical dome, for tropical butterflies, forms the eye of the butterfly, with great chalk banks representing the antennae. The proboscis is a spiral walk to a garden dedicated to Miriam Rothschild, where all her favourite nectar plants will grow. A vast hedged garden, similar to a tameflower meadow, forms the palps of the butterfly's head.

It is hoped there will be exhibitions of different kinds of planting for butterflies in a garden shaped like a caterpillar. A Butterfly Conservation Garden is planned. Even the car park will be planted up for butterflies and moths. (For more information, see the web address at the back of the book.)

ABOVE *Chalkhill Blue*.
BELOW *Adonis Blue*.

Chalkhill Blue

There are three resident British butterflies that lay their eggs on horseshoe vetch. They are the Dingy Skipper and the Chalkhill and Adonis Blue. The Dingy Skipper, although it does use horseshoe vetch, more often lays on bird's-foot trefoil. The two blues use horseshoe vetch exclusively. They are colonial butterflies and reputed to colonise new habitat very slowly. However, possibly as a result of global warming, they now appear to find new sites more quickly than they did in the past.

If you live within a few miles of colonies of these blues there may be a chance that a large south-facing bank full of horseshoe vetch will attract them. The Adonis is a little trickier than the Chalkhill Blue as it has two broods a year. Both blues are dependant on red ants, which protect the caterpillars from various predators. The Adonis overwinters as a caterpillar and does best on very warm slopes, where the ground heats up early in the year. These slopes are also ideal for red ants and the warmth will make them active early, when the caterpillar needs them.

The Chalkhill overwinters as an egg. This hatches in April, when the weather is warmer and the ants are more active. For this reason, the Chalkhill can thrive in a longer sward than the Adonis.

If you are creating a bank for the Adonis, go to some length to create very well-drained areas at the top. This will ensure low growth of plants there. If the top of the bank is cut regularly with shears – outside the egg-laying period, of course – this will also help create the short sward that is needed. Leave the cuttings on the ground for a few days.

The Chalkhill will lay on luxuriant growths of horseshoe vetch, but prefers short sprigs growing over chalk rubble. A good strategy is to cut back the foodplant around the end of June, when the butterfly is safely hidden as a chrysalis. The cut vetch will then be freshly sprouting by the time the adults emerge towards the end of July.

Scrub and Woodland

In the wild, many of the best butterfly habitats are found within scrub. Such sites are at their best during those few years when the scrub is threatening to turn into woodland. This is while there is plenty of shelter but before it becomes too shady for butterflies. Butterflies that do well in this sort of habitat – such as the Duke of Burgundy – used to have plenty of opportunity to move to sites at the right stage of development. However, as management practices changed, many of these habitats became overgrown or were grubbed out and 'improved'.

We can arrest the scrub on our own land by cutting it back every few years to create sheltered suntraps. If you have a large area of land – or even a big garden – you could consider having an area of scrub and woodland. The ideal progression of habitat would then be: butterfly garden – pond – wetland – meadow – short grassland – bank – long grass – scrub – woodland. There is no reason why you cannot incorporate some of this sequence into even a small garden.

The scrub element could be created by planting many of the shrubs we have already talked about, plus any of those mentioned below.

If there is room, the scrub could then give way to woodland. In this scrub and woodland area all the butterflies we talked about in Chapter 2 would flourish, and so could another, very secretive, group of butterflies – the Hairstreaks (see page 140).

Specialist nurseries will provide tree whips at low prices if they are bought in reasonable numbers. My own method of planting trees is usually to just stick them in the ground and let them get on with it. Some are damaged by deer (there are no rabbits in my meadow) and, although I lose a few saplings, most seem to survive. Commercial woodlands would be horrified by this approach; they use tree guards and stakes to protect the trees until they are established and a reasonable height.

The environmental charity, Landlife, has developed a method for creating woodland that fits in well with the various techniques outlined in this book. By deep ploughing they invert the soil, so the topsoil is buried and the subsoil comes to the surface. Trees are deep rooting and will find the richer soils buried below; meanwhile they will not have to face competition from coarse grasses that would grow in the topsoil. A typical wildflower mix could be sown in the subsoil, to provide interest until the trees begin to shade out any ground flora.

This works well if you are making a large wood. In smaller areas you can use the digger which is stripping topsoil to also invert the soils for your woodland. Some of the topsoil excavated while creating the meadow could also be hidden here.

You don't want the woodland area to shade any of your habitats, so the best place for it is on the north side of your property. Plant the trees for hairstreaks (see page 140) but also remember the moths. Almost all native trees have a number of moth larvae that feed on their leaves, but oak, willow and birch are thought to be host to the greatest range of species.

Scrub
Blackthorn (can be invasive), broom (best on neutral and acidic soils), bird cherry, crab apple, dog rose, dogwood, elder, gorse, guelder rose, hawthorn, holly, honeysuckle, hops, ivy, purging buckthorn, spindle, wayfaring tree and wild privet.

Scrub for wet soils
Alder buckthorn, aspen and various willows

ABOVE *Wych elm (foodplant of the White-letter Hairstreak) and blackthorn (foodplant of the Brown Hairstreak) in flower.*
LEFT *All the habitats; garden – pond – wetland – meadow – short grassland – bank – long grass – scrub – woodland.*

ABOVE *Green Hairstreak.*
BELOW *Purple Hairstreak.*

HAIRSTREAKS

GREEN Hairstreak

Another colonial butterfly that it is possible to attract to mounds and scraped areas is the Green Hairstreak. All the hairstreaks are rather elusive. Other hairstreaks flit around in the tops of trees, which accounts for their being seldom seen. The Green, although frequenting woods and scrubby areas, is found nearer ground level. I have a small colony in my meadow but I seldom see more than three or four individuals in a year. The time I usually see them is when females are on egg-laying flights. They investigate bushy patches of bird's-foot trefoil growing in sparse grassland. They also lay on dyer's greenweed and rockrose, and I have seen a single female laying on all three species. In large parts of the country, their main foodplant is gorse. I have quite a few gorse bushes but have yet to see a Green Hairstreak anywhere near them.

Tony Leibert lives near a large stretch of moor where gorse is abundant. The Green Hairstreaks that come into his garden all lay on gorse, even though other foodplants are available. You need to grow the foodplant that your local Green Hairstreaks are using.

The type of habitat that this butterfly likes has patches of very sparse grassland next to areas of longer grassland, and south-facing banks with plenty of shrubs to help create shelter. The other Hairstreaks lead a more arboreal existence.

PURPLE Hairstreak

One of the commonest unseen butterflies in Britain is the Purple Hairstreak. This is because it usually spends its time high up on the canopy of oaks. It is found over large parts of Britain, even near the centre of London. Colonies of Purple Hairstreaks can be found on the same oaks, or even single oak, for generations.

Almost 30 years ago, Tony Liebert planted oaks and now has the Purple Hairstreak on them. The oaks need to be planted with ash, as the adults sip honeydew (a sweet substance secreted by aphids) that is often found abundantly on ash.

You need to plan ahead a little if you want to encourage this butterfly, but it may be already present in your neighbourhood without your knowing it. Michael Fuller, in his book, *Butterflies of Wiltshire*, describes the process of finding and counting these butterflies. During the day the butterflies wander from leaf to leaf, sipping honeydew and rarely seen from the ground. In the early evening, if it is calm and warm, they fly around the treetops playing tag. You could investigate your local oaks – use binoculars – at about seven o'clock in the evening around mid-July: you may find that you've had hairstreaks all along.

When planting your oaks you have to imagine how much sunlight they will get in 15-20 years' time, as the trees need to be in full sun for a large part of the day. There is no point in planting them on the north side of existing tall trees.

At Ryewater one year, during a very warm spell, hundreds of Purple Hairstreaks descended from their oaks in the coppice, and were found on the tops of alder buckthorn. The coppice is a large plantation of native species, with alder buckthorn interplanted between many other shrubs. We found the insects on no species of tree other than alder blackthorn. They may have been after honeydew but otherwise we have no idea why they behaved like this.

WHITE-LETTER Hairstreak

This is another hairstreak that spends its life up in the treetops. Again, you need to plan ahead for this species, as it lays its eggs on elm. This butterfly lost a lot of its breeding grounds when Dutch elm disease killed so many of Britain's elms. Fortunately, there is evidence to suggest that wych elm is the favourite elm species, and this tree does not succumb to the disease as easily as English and other elms.

Although White-letters will lay on saplings, it is generally flowering elms that are used. I planted wych elms in rich topsoil and they reached flowering size in six to seven years. Plant the trees on the south side of existing trees for the best chance of attracting this butterfly. It is scarcer than the Purple and you have to regard yourself as fortunate if it sets up home in your trees. If you are going to plant trees anyway, why not some wych elm? There is work going on now to find disease-resistant English elms and they may be available soon. There is also an attractive weeping elm available for smaller gardens, *Ulmus glabra* 'Camperdownii'.

BROWN Hairstreak

This is a scarce insect, sighted in only a few scattered areas, mostly in the south and west of Britain. Check the distribution maps to find out if you live where colonies of Brown Hairstreak are found. If you do, the good news is that you have a high chance of attracting the butterfly to your garden. The bad news is that you probably won't see it even when it does come visiting. The female Brown Hairstreak lays her eggs on blackthorn and other closely-related shrubs. She generally chooses one-year-old wood. Tony Leibert has planted a 70m-long blackthorn hedge, which, when cut, is about 1.5m high. Each year, after the leaves have fallen, he searches for the butterflies' eggs. One year as many as 90 were found. Most of the eggs are 'where the new growths of the year emerge from those of the previous year or where spines or buds are present on new growths'. Tony cuts his hedge by hand, taking it back to 3-4cm or so above the last cut. Cut stems with eggs attached are laid carefully on top of the hedge.

In the countryside, many eggs are lost because of the way hedges are cut today. Butterfly Conservation can be contacted to find out the best ways for farmers to manage hedgerows in areas where the Brown Hairstreak is present.

TOP *White-letter Hairstreak.*
ABOVE *Brown Hairstreak.*
LEFT *Brown Hairstreak eggs are easier to find than the adults. The eggs are tiny, about three times the size of the full stop at the end of this sentence. Search for them during the winter months.*

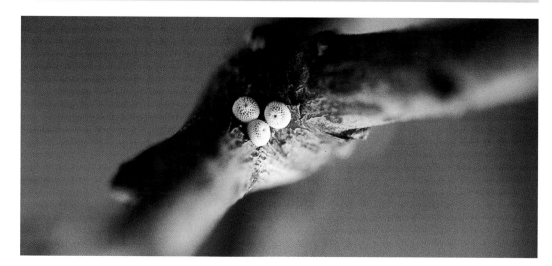

Chapter Nine

Falling into the Moth Trap

Many years ago, I met Mike Bailey and we discovered that we shared many of the same interests. Mike was a very keen bird watcher and also a potter. Years later we met by chance. I found out that, whereas I had moved towards the light, Mike had gone towards the dark. His passion now was moths.

There has always been a small element of rivalry between 'butterfly people' and 'moth people'. Butterflies are glamorous; moths are creepy: that is the perception. Butterflies often get all the attention, with moths just tagged on at the end. In my case, it is the visual that excites me, and it tends to be rather dark when most moths are out and about. But this is no

RIGHT *The Robinson moth trap.*
BELOW *The Poplar Hawkmoth. Part of the Moth Gallery exhibiting a plethora of form, pattern, shape, colour and texture.*

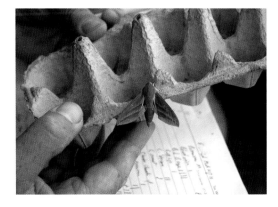

excuse when moths are examined closely. There are moths with bright colours and moths with more subtle colouration but, though the majority are browns, greys, creams and delicate greens, it is the intricate patterns that these colours form, together with the multitude of different wing and antennae shapes, that are so endlessly fascinating.

It is this that inspires Mike Bailey. He is a keen ornithologist and he was studying some reed beds, important for reed warblers, sedge warblers and other birds, that were being ravaged. It was suggested that a moth might be responsible for the devastation and a friend brought along a lamp to trap night-flying insects. They caught many and finally discovered that a moth called the Twin-spotted Wainscot was causing the damage. But in the process Mike was caught in the 'trap'.

He bought one of the blue actinic lamps and has been trapping moths in his own garden ever since. The many forms of moth, the chance of finding a moth new to the county or even country, and the opportunity to do this pioneering work from his own back garden has captivated him for the last 20 years. I was invited along for a moth-trapping evening (and morning).

The trap he uses now is a Robinson moth trap. This mercury vapour lamp is favoured by many moth-ers. It creates a strong light and needs to be placed where it will not disturb neighbours. For those just starting, Mike recommends the actinic light: the light it emits is less intense and it has the advantages that it can be run off a car battery and is easily transported. The Robinson trap runs off the electric mains. You will need a generator to use it in open countryside.

Mike's light is timed to go on at a certain time so he does not normally need to set it up. As I was there, however, we went out together to watch the first moths coming in. The day had been warm, perfect weather for butterflies, but the temperature was falling. Warm, cloudy nights are best for moths. The lamp was switched on, then we left. When we returned, a maelstrom of insects was around the light. Among them, large moths of many kinds turned frenzied loops. I tried to take pictures of the moths whirling around, but failed.

Normally, Mike gets up at daybreak to count and then release the moths, but we agreed to meet later in the morning. (Birds get used to a morning feed of moths if the catch is released during the day, hence the usual early rise.) At about 9am, the count began. At the base of the moth trap there are a number of egg boxes and the moths collect under these. There is a debate in the moth world about the types of egg boxes to use. Some moth-ers do not like the boxes with the pointy egg holders as the moths can get trapped at the point, and are then difficult to extract.

Each box is turned over. The moths sit patiently as they are counted. I had expected a buzz of wings but very few move at all in the daylight. Most of the moths are silver, grey or brown, but some are real beauties. I often find Elephant Hawkmoth caterpillars but I had never seen the adult, with its exquisite colouring of faded rose-pink and old gold verging on yellow ochre. The Buff Tips were fun. These moths look remarkably like a freshly-cut section of small twig. The pattern that mimics the 'cut' even appears to show the sap wood.

While counting, Mike found a moth that interested him and slipped it into a small plastic vial to identify later. It was probably a Burnished Brass, he explained, but just recently it had been found that the Burnished Brass was not one species but two, distinguishable only by their genitalia. Mike has now become an expert in moth genitalia and gets moths sent through the post for him to identify by examining them through a small optical microscope. Some of the photographs of these moths taken through the microscope are stunning.

After the count is made, the results are sent to the County Moth Recorder.

FROM TOP *Elephant Hawkmoth; the Buff Tip; keeping a moth for identification.*

Keeping detailed records allows Mike Bailey to prepare graphs.

'This graph RIGHT explains the fluctuations in population of the Ingrailed Clay. Most moth species' annual totals go up and down in a rather erratic manner. The Ingrailed Clay population seems to rise and fall in a remarkably predictable way. The graph shows the numbers seen since 1989, revealing a smooth oscillation in numbers each year. I suspect, although it is unclear, who or what the predator is, that this is an example of an oscillating predator-prey relationship.

For this species, it seems to be operating on a seven to eight year cycle, in which the predators gradually reduce the moth population. Then, due to the absence of a host, the predators die off and the moth number can increase again. A well-known example of this type of predator-prey relationship is the Holly Blue butterfly, which cycles with the ichneumon wasp. The forecast for 2007 to 2009 would be for low years, with annual totals to peak around 2011 or 2012.'

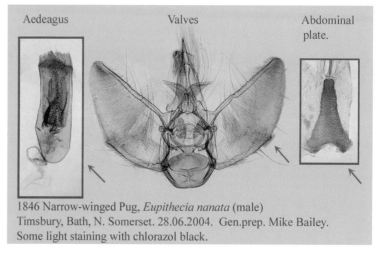

Ingrailed Clay. Timsbury

(Bar chart values by year: 1989: 167, 1990: 150, 1991: 93, 1992: 61, 1993: 28, 1994: 16, 1995: 16, 1996: 75, 1997: 122, 1998: 64, 1999: 68, 2000: 40, 2001: 20, 2002: 97, 2003: 130, 2004: 154, 2005: 120, 2006: 46. X-axis: Years)

1846 Narrow-winged Pug, *Eupithecia nanata* (male)
Timsbury, Bath, N. Somerset. 28.06.2004. Gen.prep. Mike Bailey.
Some light staining with chlorazol black.

(Labels: Aedeagus, Valves, Abdominal plate.)

RIGHT *Photograph through the optical microscope.*

Mullein Moth caterpillar.

MOTHS IN THE GARDEN

All the created habitats described earlier in the book will also attract moths. So many food-plants are the foodplants of moths that only a few can be mentioned here. See Recommended Reading (page 190) for books that go into greater detail. Generally, wild plants are best, but there is a wide range of garden plants that moths also like. Fruit trees and currant bushes that are closely related to their wild cousins are – to the consternation of many gardeners – greatly appreciated. Even the leyland cypress, now much used in hedge planting, has associated moths: three moths from the Mediterranean have moved into Britain because of the extensive planting of this cypress here.

Willowherbs will attract the Elephant Hawkmoth (so-called because the caterpillar looks like an elephant's trunk). These plants are not ones that are normally suitable for a meadow as they more often favour recently disturbed ground. The willowherb that might fit into your meadow if you have a pond or wet spot is the great willowherb, sometimes known as codlins and cream; I regularly find Elephant Hawkmoth caterpillars in my patch of this in the meadow. There is a white form of the rosebay willowherb, *Epilobium angustifolium* 'Album', which looks

Day-flying Moths

As you walk through the garden or meadow, every now and then you disturb a butterfly-like insect. Was it a butterfly or a moth? Many moths, when disturbed like this, fly a little way, crash-land into a clump of vegetation, and close their wings on landing. It's hard to mark where they are. Butterflies, on the other hand, stay in the light and are far easier to see from a distance. Butterflies also seem more expert in flight; some even glide. But there are some moths that are just as much at home in the daylight as butterflies, fly with just as much panache, and may be just as brightly coloured. These are the day-flying moths.

The Five-spot Burnet and Six-spot Burnet are two of these. Their dramatic black and scarlet colouring, coupled with their large black antennae, mark them out as the meadow's extroverts. There are a few different variations and subspecies of the Five-spot, and a closely-related species, the Narrow-bordered Five-spot. They are all colonial.

The Five-spot emerges first. It likes wetter areas than the Six-spot. In my meadow both species, but especially the Five-spot, seem to have something like a boom and bust cycle. One evening, at the end of June 2000, I counted over 60 Five-spots roosting on a few large clumps of knapweed flowers. During the day they whizz about but, as the evening draws on, they are like clockwork toys that have almost wound down, each sitting on or under a knapweed flower head. The next year I did not see any. By 2006, their numbers had recovered. As with the Holly Blue, it is probable that a parasite is regulating their numbers.

The Six-spot emerges a month later but in much larger numbers. The flight of the Six-spot is very direct and fast, slightly reminiscent of a helicopter. It spends a lot of time nectaring so there needs to be plenty of flowers. The Six-spot lays its eggs on bird's-foot trefoil (and other legumes) and seems to like bushy plants. Their striped caterpillars are easy to see: they are poisonous and birds learn to dislike them, so they can afford to be noticed, both as moth and caterpillar. The Six-spot rarely leaves the bank where the majority of its nectar and foodplants grow, and the Five-spot seems to fly only in the hay meadow.

The Chimney Sweeper is a jaunty little day-flying moth whose caterpillars feed on pignut. It is one of my favourites but would be difficult to attract to a created meadow as it is problematical to establish the slow-growing pignut.

In June, the Burnet Companion, another whose foodplant is bird's-foot trefoil, may cause confusion. From a distance, a freshly-emerged specimen can look a little like a Duke of Burgundy, and an old worn one like a Dingy Skipper. Huge numbers of these moths can be found in some meadows. Others to look out for are the Mother Shipton, the Silver Y, the Cinnabar and the Hummingbird Hawkmoth.

The Scarlet Tiger, another of the brilliant day-flying moths, seems to be spreading northwards and is commonly reported in some gardens. A similar moth, the Jersey Tiger, has a toehold in Dorset, but could also spread northwards following global warming.

very attractive in gardens.

Another moth which I only see as a caterpillar is the Mullein moth. It is remarkable how quickly they can eat up a one and a half metre-high common mullein. I grow common and dark mullein and, although the Mullein moth is attracted to both, there seems to be a preference for the common mullein.

In the garden, mulleins that have been consumed by this moth can look very unattractive. A solution is to have one sacrificial mullein and put all the caterpillars on it. Or if you

TOP *Five-spot on knapweed.*
ABOVE: *Mating pairs of Six-spot.*

are determined to protect all your mulleins, try the caterpillars on buddleia, which they also like.

Nectar plants that attract butterflies will also attract moths, but a number of flowers open in the evening or at night and are of particular value to moths. Many of these plants are white and in the gloaming seem luminous. White jasmine, sweet rocket, night-scented stock, honeysuckle, evening primrose and the tobacco plant are some of the best.

Cinnabar caterpillars on ragwort.

The Mint moth on germander speedwell. This tiny micro-moth could appear in your garden if you grow lots of marjoram.

The Burnet Companion.

A Design for a Small Garden

Now that we have reached the end of the habitat creation section, let us see how much butterfly-friendly habitat we can squeeze into a small garden. Low-fertility gardening is low-maintenance gardening, as well as attracting butterflies and many other forms of wildlife. The design on the next page incorporates many of the features discussed throughout the book.

The meadow is divided into eight different areas. The most important plants for butterflies are listed for each area, though many more could be grown.

In this design, the topsoil is removed from the central area of the garden and placed around the east west and north side. If it can be buried, so much the better. The paths should have some kind of mat underlay. Matting could also be used under the bay area, as an easy way of forming a barrier between the topsoil and any substrates you use. The bay is made by either the limestone chippings method or by putting down a layer of rubble, followed by any of the substrates available locally.

The mounds are made by capping a pile of rubble with limestone of some kind. If limestone is in short supply, only use it on the south side of the mound and cover the north side with anything that is available.

The paths are made with gravel or chippings or whatever you can get your hands on. However, the contrast of white kibbled chalk with the dark greens of fescues and vetches is highly attractive. Whatever substrate you use, it needs to be at least 10cm (4in) deep, preferably more. You can give the paths a straight clean edge or allow fine grasses, vetches, wild strawberry and other plants to grow into the substrate, creating a wilder look.

Butterfly plants could be also grown in containers on the patio. (See Chapters 1 and 2 for more ideas.)

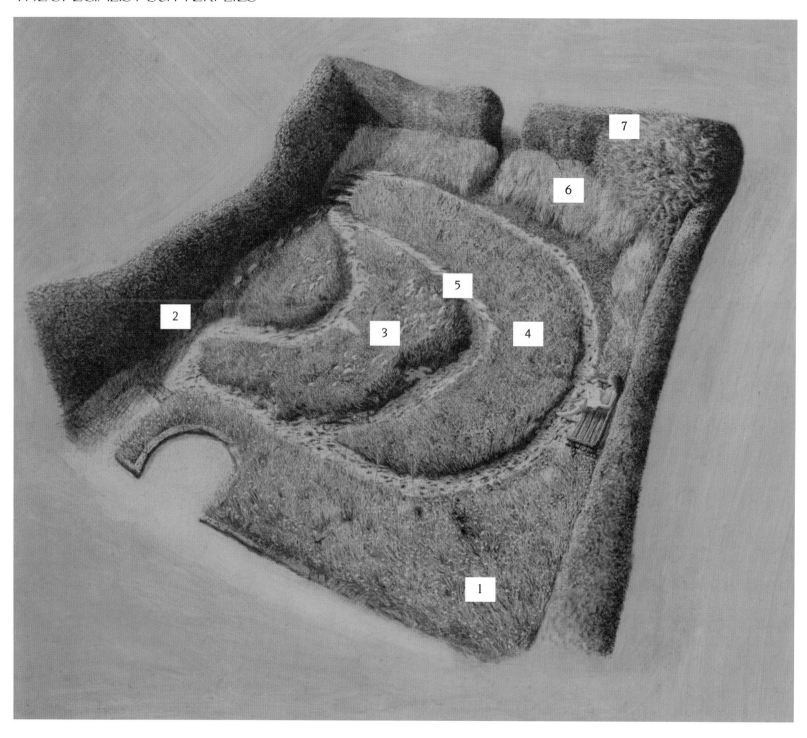

Planning a small butterfly-friendly garden

1. Tameflower meadow next to the house. See Chapter 1 for principle plants. This could also be a wildflower meadow, with the usual range of wild flowers but especially knapweed and sorrel, and a wide range of wild grasses.

2. Violet and primrose bank. Principle plants: violets and primroses, but could include other woodland plants such as bluebells, red campion, greater stitchwort and bugle.

3. Chalk or limestone mounds managed with one to two cuts a year. Principle plants: horseshoe vetch, kidney vetch, bird's-foot trefoil, wild strawberry, rockrose, hairy violet, marjoram, wild thyme and sheep's fescue. The emphasis here is on foodplants.

4. Limestone chippings, or other substrate, managed with one cut a year. Principle plants: marjoram, small, Devil's-bit and field scabious, greater knapweed, viper's bugloss, sorrel and sheep's fescue. The emphasis in this area is on nectar plants.

5. Path made with kibbled chalk, limestone chippings or gravel. Principle plants are the same as for the mounds, with the addition of sorrel.

6. Long grass. Principle plants: cocksfoot, Yorkshire fog, red fescue, smooth meadow grass and other meadow grasses; knapweed. To make the long grass looking tidy, keep the grass below the coarse grass clumps very short.

7. Trees and hedgerow. Principle plants: at least one buddleia and one buckthorn as free-standing trees; hops, holly, ivy, blackthorn, oak and others kept as a closely cut, rounded hedge

8. Pond or bog garden for purple loosestrife and other wetland plants.

Part Four:
Butterfly Conservation

Chapter Ten

Growing Plants for Butterflies

There are many plants that butterflies like to nectar on and many early flowering meadow plants are good nectar plants. Lesser celandine, dandelion, bluebell, buttercup, the hawkbits, ox-eye daisy, ladies smock and ragged robin can all flower profusely. But at the time they are flowering, there are few butterflies about. Just one may be seen nectaring on sheets of buttercup. Later in the year, numbers of butterflies begin to build and there may be many on one plant. In the selection of nectar plants below, later flowering plants are given prominence. The foodplants are a more fixed group, with many butterflies favouring only one species of plant. Some butterflies, for example the Green Hairstreak, lay on a number of plant species.

RIGHT *Dyer's greenweed; one of the many foodplants of the Green Hairstreak.*

PREVIOUS PAGES *Two butterflies, one common and one extinct. The Small Tortoiseshell is still a common butterfly over most of Britain. In the 19th century, the Large Tortoiseshell, although never as common, could still be found in reasonable numbers in the south of Britain. Although occasional specimens still turn up, it is now regarded as extinct in Britain as a breeding butterfly.*

A Meadow Brown on the wonderfully-named corky-fruited water dropwort, which flowers in June. This plant is found in the South West. Where it flowers, it flowers profusely.

GROW YOUR OWN

After propagating wildflowers for many years, long enough to know that I dislike pricking out seedlings into individual pots and caring for them, I have developed a method that involves the minimum amount of effort but produces the maximum number of plants.

Seed Collection

Wildflower seed is ready for collection at different times of the year. In general, wildflowers that flower early in the year take longer for their seed to ripen than those that flower late. Cowslip seed is ripe by early July, a couple of months after flowering, whereas some Devil's-bit scabious seed will be ripe in late August while other Devil's-bit is still flowering. Ripening speeds up towards the end of the season, with only some seed ready in early July but most ripe by August.

One way of raising plants, particularly plants for seed, is to grow them through mats. First lay down a mat – geotextile matting is the type to use – over fertile soil. The dark material will kill off any vegetation growing underneath. Then you cut small slits in the matting and plant through into the fertile topsoil. If you want the matting to last a long time, use the best quality material. This will be translucent, though, and let the light through, allowing plants under the mat to grow. A fine covering of soil or gravel will prevent this, and also allow you to grow low-growing plants, such as wild strawberry. They will scramble about at the feet of the larger plants.

Because plants growing like this have no competition they grow quite large and provide lots of seed or offshoots. Violets raised this way produce runners vigorously. If you are growing Devil's-bit scabious they also attract a lot of nectaring butterflies in the late summer.

Large and small seed trays with the edge of the raised bed in view.

SOWING

It is best to sow seed as soon as you have collected it. If you have to keep seed for a later project, dry it out on a window ledge first before storing it somewhere dry and cool.

Use peatless soil compost in your seed tray and fill to within a couple of centimetres of the tray's rim. But do not buy ordinary seed trays, which are shallow and dry out quickly: buy the large trays that are used to hold plant pots, and drill holes in their base to allow drainage. A large tray holds moisture far better and you can leave the plants to grow on in them far longer than in standard seed trays. When sowing, small seed can be scattered on the surface of the compost; larger seed should be pressed down into it. Then cover the seed tray with a sheet of glass and place in a greenhouse.

My greenhouse is a small lean-to on the north side of my shed. This keeps the trays out of direct sunshine. If you do not have a greenhouse you could rig up a small shelter with a sheet of plastic corrugated roofing.

Most seeds germinate in the spring. When you see seedlings starting to emerge, remove the glass. Leave the plants to develop in their trays, still keeping them out of direct light. They will only need watering occasionally in these large containers, but keep your eye on them. If you only want to grow a few plants then this is the moment to prick out some of the seedlings into individual pots.

I used to grow on plants in a flowerbed, but they would get lost, eaten or forgotten. I now use a high raised bed. This is made with large paving slabs, held in place by fence posts to form a huge container. Fill the bed almost to the top with topsoil. (It works well if you can do two jobs at once, make a small meadow by stripping the topsoil and use that soil to make a bank or raised bed.) There may be roots of bindweed in the soil; if so, when the bed is nearly full, cover it with some sort of porous matting to keep the roots down. Finally, fill the top 10cm (4in) with sterilized compost, so there are no weed seeds.

Position this bed in the semi-shade to cut down on watering and to protect seedlings from direct sunlight. When ready to transfer seedlings from a seed tray, just scoop out hand-fuls of compost and seedlings and snuggle them down into the compost of the raised bed. There is no pricking out involved. Sometimes the seedlings' roots have formed their own dense matrix in the tray so that everything comes out in one piece. This can be pulled apart and the separate portions planted in the bed.

When these clumps of plants grow larger they can be scooped up again – easy with loose compost – and broken into smaller clumps for replanting. This may be repeated two or three times but is quick work.

In the autumn or the following spring the plants will be ready to be put out in their final position. Choose a period of wet weather for this.

THE PLANTS

Agrimony. Sow in seed trays in the autumn; it will germinate in the spring. This is one of the foodplants of the Grizzled Skipper. In common with the other foodplants of rare and localized butterflies, it is far more attractive to the butterfly if it is growing in sparse or bare ground. It will germinate fairly successfully if sown directly into the soil in the autumn, as long as there is not much competition from other plants.

The larger cousin of agrimony, fragrant agrimony, likes a little more fertility and is a plant for the hedgerow or more fertile meadow.

Agrimony: the seeds stick to clothing and animal fur.

Betony. Betony germinates best if the seed tray is left out over the winter. It is quite a good nectar plant, but also a sturdy plant that will stand a lot of mistreatment. It is the star of the show in my meadow. If you can grow it in your meadow then grow masses of it. It does not like to grow in tall grasses – a low to medium turf suits it best. Again, it will germinate well if sown into areas that have been stripped of their topsoil.

Betony supported by field scabious.

Bird's-foot Trefoil. This is the major foodplant of the Common Blue and the Dingy Skipper. Some day-flying moths, especially the Six-spot Burnets and the Burnet Companion, use it as well. Bird's-foot trefoil is also a good nectar plant. It can be sown directly into bare ground and is part of most meadow mixtures. If you have difficulty getting it to germinate in the meadow, grow it in seed trays for planting out later.

Bird's-foot trefoil, nectar and foodplant par excellence.

As with all legumes, bird's-foot trefoil has the ability to fix atmospheric nitrogen and so supply nitrogen to the soil, making it more fertile. The plant also has a long taproot which enables it to grow bushy and crowd out lower-growing plants. It looks best growing in very poor soils where it stays small and flowers more profusely. For this reason, it might be best to be cautious about sowing a lot of it on some soils. If you want to limit it to certain areas, it has most use to the Common Blue in hot spots like the edges of paths. The day-flying moths are not so fussy.

If bird's-foot trefoil is growing strongly, it might be worth cutting some patches in early June. These will regrow and be more to the liking of the second brood of Common Blue. Leave the cuttings for a day or two to, allow any caterpillars time to crawl off them.

Bladder Campion. This grows easily from seed sown in seed trays in the spring. Along with a close relative, nodding catchfly, it is a good nectar plant for moths.

A number of moth caterpillars feed on the seed heads of bladder campion.

Bramble. Although many of us would be not be happy to grow bramble, it can be one of the best nectar plants. Some brambles seem to attract more butterflies than others. This may be due to their position in the garden, or to their particular micro-species. There are cultivated brambles grown for their berries, which might be more appropriate in the formal garden.

Commas on bramble.

Broom and Gorse. These, and the other shrubs and trees, can be bought from nurseries specializing in native trees and shrubs. I have had only limited success with cuttings of broom pushed into the ground *in situ*; prickly gorse may well be as difficult.

Broom in flower.

Buddleia. Buddleia needs to grow in a well-drained soil. Like privet, it grows quite well from large cuttings left in the ground over the winter. If you have difficulty with it, try planting it on raised mounds where there is plenty of free-draining material.

Buddleia hedge made from cuttings.

Bugle.

Bugle. Bugle prefers damp, bare ground in semi-shady situations, but will also grow and spread in full sun. Its runners soon turn a single plant into many. It is a good nectar plant for early on in the year.

Cowslip and Primrose. Both germinate readily if left out over the winter in seed trays. Sow the seed as soon as it is ripe. You cannot have too many cowslips: it is one of the plants I try to sow every year (along with betony and Devil's-bit scabious). It can be planted all over the meadow but prefers areas of shorter or fine grasses.

Primrose.

Primrose, besides being a woodland plant, will also grow in north- or east-facing banks or in semi-shade –

under a bush or at the edge of the meadow next to a hedge – where there is more moisture.

Yellow cowslips with wood anenome.

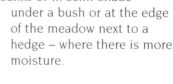

Cranesbill. With perennials such as meadow cranesbill, scarify the seed and sow in seed trays. With the biennials and annuals, scatter the seed in the autumn. Cut-leaved cranesbill seed is not available commercially but it is a common plant and can be collected by hand in small amounts in July. Sow it in sparse or bare areas.

Cut-leaved cranesbill.

156

Meadow cranesbill is large enough to compete with the coarse grasses in a fertile meadow and makes a stunning show there. It is a long-lived perennial, usually found in calcareous soils. Even if your soil is low in lime, it is still worth planting.

Crosswort. Crosswort is of no direct benefit to butterflies, but is useful to the meadow-maker because it can successfully compete with grasses. By scrambling over them for a few seasons it forms, if it is not cut, quite a large patch. At this stage you can plant robust wildflowers such as valerian through it. You can also pull it up by the handful and push it where you want it: as long as there is enough moisture, it will grow.

Crosswort. Each flower is a small cross.

Dyer's Greenweed. This is a plant that can take some time to raise as it grows slowly. Scarify the seed first and let the winter's cold get to it. It should germinate in the spring. It can be sown in areas where the topsoil has been stripped. With little competition, it germinates well. An easier way to propagate it is with cuttings taken in early summer. Take a cutting with a heel, strip off most of the leaves (including any flower buds), and dip the heel in rooting hormone. Put the cuttings in a flowerpot filled with half sand, half compost and place in a polythene bag to prevent it drying out. Keep the pot out of direct sunlight, preferably under cover.

Dyer's greenweed. A yellow dye is made from this plant that mixes with the blue of woad to make a green dye.

An even easier method is to fill a large, deep flowerpot with clay, packing it tightly into the pot. Take cuttings of dyer's greenweed and, with a screwdriver, create deep holes in the clay, then place the cuttings in them. Use the screwdriver to pack the clay tightly back around the cuttings. You should be able to get a large number into each pot. Place the pot out of direct sunlight, in a small tray of water.

I have also had success with putting the cuttings directly in the ground. This works well after the ground has been stripped of its topsoil and there is little competition from other plants; it must be done at a time when the ground is moist.

Expect your success rate to vary from year to year. Spiny restharrow can be treated in the same way, though with less success. I find it germinates well from seed sown after topsoil stripping.

Fleabane. A plant that supplies nectar in late summer, fleabane spreads by underground runner and if you grow it in the flower border there will be new plants to dig up each year. April and early May are generally good months for transplanting species that spread vegetatively, as the new plants will be up by then but the soil is still moist, so you do not have to worry about watering. Dig up the plantlet with 7–10cm (3–4in) of the underground runner, and transplant to the desired position.

Fleabane, one of the Small Copper's favourite nectar plants.

Garlic mustard, sometimes described as a roadside plant.

Garlic Mustard. Germinates easily if sown in pots or directly into soil in a semi-shady position.

Grasses and Sedges. Grasses and sedges grow well from seed sown directly into the ground. There is a patch of glaucous sedge in my meadow that only came to my notice recently. I thought it had arrived by itself, then I remembered collecting some seed from a roadside verge four or five years earlier and sowing it directly into the meadow. Some seeds are slow starters.

Like most grasses, sheep's fescue is best introduced in seed form.

Hops attracts many insects, besides the Comma.

Small Blue nectaring on horseshoe vetch.

Herb Robert. This is usually a plant of shady areas but it will also grow in limestone banks and scree. Scatter some seed in the bank to provide nectar for some of the early white butterflies.

Hops. Collect hop seed in autumn, sow it in seed trays and cover with glass. Do not spend too long trying to separate the seed from the flower-like seed cases: it will germinate in the spring, cleaned or not. In the right situation, the vigorous hop goes over the top, literally.

Horseshoe Vetch. Although this vetch grows reasonably easily from seed – if you scarify it first and then sow it in seed trays – the seed is quite expensive. It is a fussy plant, liking poor, well-drained and usually limey soil, and there may well only be limited ground to grow it on (the very infertile area or the limestone mounds). I would recommend initially buy-

GROWING PLANTS FOR BUTTERFLIES

ing plugs from a professional grower and in later years collecting seed from your own plants. It can also be propagated by taking cuttings from the woody part of the plant (see Rockrose).

Horseshoe vetch is the foodplant of the Adonis Blue, the Chalkhill Blue and sometimes the Dingy Skipper. These three insects are fairly scarce now and the two blues, especially, are highly colonial and would be unlikely to take up residence in your meadow unless it was near a south-facing chalky hillside. A lot of nurseries and seed houses give the impression that all you have to do is plant some violets and horseshoe vetch, then Fritillaries and Chalkhill Blues will come winging in. They will not, but I would still recommend planting horseshoe vetch, for a number of reasons. One of the best ways of learning to recognize a plant in the wild is to grow it. And they are bonny plants, especially when grown in great rafts. There is also the faint hope that one day one of the rarities will turn up and start a colony in your meadow. The best reason, though, it is one of the best nectar plants.

Kidney vetch.

Kidney Vetch. To grow kidney vetch, treat it in the same way as bird's-foot trefoil. It is a biennial and seems to germinate best in sparse, well-drained grassland, especially during and after hot summers. This means that you may have to create bare patches and sprinkle seeds from existing plants into them, otherwise it will slowly die out. Grown on limestone mounds it should, with a little help, be able to perpetuate itself.

Although normally thought of as a *calcicole*, I have found that kidney vetch will grow just about anywhere, except in wet soils. And even on wet clay it will flower, despite not thriving. I would include it in most meadow sowings, although you may find it flowers only once. If the soil is thin and you have reason to believe that it may persist, remember to sow again the following year otherwise, being a biennial, it will initially flower only every second year.

Knapweeds. Like marjoram, knapweed grows easily from seed. Also like marjoram, knapweed (greater and lesser, or hardheads) is one of the best sources of nectar. It generally flowers before marjoram and is one of the major nectar plants for butterflies whose larvae feed on grass. A lot of these insects emerge from mid-June to mid-July, when marjoram takes over as the main nectar plant. They include the Large and Small Skipper, the Meadow Brown, the Marbled White, the Ringlet and, slightly later, the Gatekeeper. These species are often the most populous in the meadow, so knapweed is a must.

Greater knapweed.

Common knapweed, or hardheads.

The knapweed in my hay meadow has almost finished flowering by the end of July, leaving few plants rich in nectar there – although there are plenty on the bank. There is a meadow nearby where knapweed flowers later than mine. I have collected a few seeds from here to grow on, in the hope that the resulting plants will provide my butterflies with nectar well into August.

Both knapweeds can be grown in the same way as marjoram. If you have a lot of seed, try sowing directly into seed drills in the border. Greater knapweed prefers well-drained soil; lesser knapweed will grow in a wide variety of soils.

159

As I explore nearby meadows, I am constantly finding plants that are flowering at different times to the plants in my own meadow. There are several possible explanations for this: height above sea level, whether the plant is in a sunny position or a windy position – all affect flowering times. But the historical management of a site may also be an influence. If a meadow is cut at the same time each year, the plants that manage to set seed before the field is mown will pass on their early-flowering characteristics. In time, the whole colony may flower earlier than the same plant species just a field away.

Marjoram.

Marjoram. This plant never fails to attract butterflies when it flowers. It needs to grow in a warm, sheltered spot, and butterflies are more likely to use it if the plant flowers above the surrounding grasses. It is easy, however, to pull up grass stalks that rise above the marjoram.

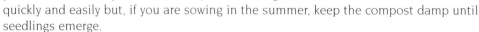

You can sow marjoram seeds at any time; it doesn't need the winter cold to help it germinate. There are thousands of seeds to the gram so you can grow more than enough for your meadow at very little cost. Marjoram seeds germinate quickly and easily but, if you are sowing in the summer, keep the compost damp until seedlings emerge.

Marjoram can also be successfully propagated vegetively. Break off a piece with a small amount of root attached and plant it in the ground. If you are growing marjoram in the flower border, dig up the whole clump, break off a biggish piece, and replant it in the hole. The remainder of the clump will provide lots of marjoram stems with roots for planting out and, by the following year, the replanted section will be almost the size of the original clump.

An abundance of marjoram may well be one of the principle reasons a passing butterfly might decide to stay in your meadow. Butterflies like the Gatekeeper strongly favour it, and the second broods of the Common Blue, the Small Copper and the Brown Argus seem equally attracted.

Narrow-leaved everlasting pea, one of the Brimstone's favoured nectar plants.

Nettles, although unpopular for their stings, can be attractive.

Narrow-leaved everlasting pea. This grows well in pots. Scarify the large seeds before sowing.

Nettles. Small Tortoiseshells, Red Admirals, Commas and Peacocks all lay their eggs on nettles, but they are fussy about the nettles they select. They generally choose nettles in a sunny, sheltered position, and prefer plants which are young and vigorous.

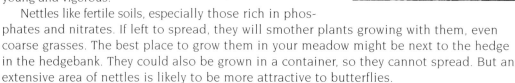

Nettles like fertile soils, especially those rich in phosphates and nitrates. If left to spread, they will smother plants growing with them, even coarse grasses. The best place to grow them in your meadow might be next to the hedge in the hedgebank. They could also be grown in a container, so they cannot spread. But an extensive area of nettles is likely to be more attractive to butterflies.

If you grow nettles, cut half of them in June, as this ensures fresh growth for egg laying.

Leave the cuttings where they fall in case there are eggs or caterpillars on them. Caterpillars can be protected from birds by throwing a light net over the patch.

Pignut. Besides providing nectar early in the summer, this plant is the foodplant of one of my favourite day-flying moths, the Chimney Sweeper. This is a small black moth with white wing tips which flies jauntily round the meadow even in cool weather.

Pignut. Children used to grub up the tubers. Pigs still do.

Pignut is a fairly common woodland plant, although it can also be found in grassland (especially ancient meadows). It does not transplant well and can take some time to reach flowering size. However, like some other umbellifers, it germinates well if sown immediately after collecting the seed. Sow it directly into the meadow area if there are plenty of bare patches.

Purging and Alder Buckthorn. Probably easiest to buy it from nurseries specializing in British trees. Whips are very cheap if bought in bulk.

Brimstone laying on the unfurling leaves of buckthorn.

Purple Loosestrife. Last year I counted 20 Speckled Woods on purple loosestrife. It is worth having a pond, no matter how small, if only to grow this plant. You can also grow it in a marshy area, along with water mint, lady's smock, hemp agrimony, valerian and ragged robin – all good butterfly plants.

Purple loosestrife and tansy.

Purple loosestrife grows reasonably easily from seed sown during the summer in compost that is kept moist. Put the seed tray in a watertight container and keep a centimetre of water in it. The seed germinates best in direct sunlight. Once you have your first plants it is very easy to detach a piece of rootstock in the spring for planting on.

Ragwort. This is the foodplant of the Cinnabar moth and an excellent nectar plant too. It is a biennial and occurs in disturbed ground. Farmers can get irate if they see one growing in your meadow, because the plant is highly poisonous to livestock if eaten in hay. You would certainly be unpopular if you let thousands of plants grow; one or two might be overlooked.

Many will recognise the Cinnabar caterpillars that feed on ragwort. Less well known is just how beautiful the Cinnabar moth is.

The close relative, hoary ragwort, is a perennial or a short-lived perennial, but little used by butterflies as a nectar plant. Hoverflies love it, though, and the Cinnabar will use it as a foodplant.

Rockrose.

Rockrose. In the south of England there is a chance of attracting the Brown Argus with rockrose. I always associate it with horseshoe vetch. They not only like the same sorts of conditions but also flower together and can be propagated in the same ways.

It is sensible to buy plugs initially: seed is expensive and it is anyway a tricky plant to grow from seed. After a year or two plugs will have grown into bushy plants and you can start taking cuttings from them. Select sturdy material. If you are growing them in a limestone mound you can stick the cuttings straight into the limey ground where you want them to grow. This needs to be done in the autumn or early in the year so you can be sure there will be enough moisture for the cuttings to root.

Rockrose and horseshoe vetch seed can be gathered together. Scarify the seed and sow it in large seed trays soon after you have collected it. Some of it will germinate before the winter and some in spring. Only a small percentage of the seed germinates at this point; the remainder may germinate in subsequent years. If you continue to use the same large seed tray to sow rockrose and horseshoe vetch those seeds that have not germinated one year may well germinate the next.

RIGHT FROM TOP *Devil's-bit scabious; Field scabious; Small scabious.*
BELOW *Sorrel.*

Scabious. All three scabious (small, field and Devil's-bit) germinate well if left in a seed tray over winter. These are plants to plant wherever they will thrive. Devil's-bit is the most versatile and, besides being the foodplant of the Marsh Fritillary, also one of the best nectar plants for late in the year when most of the other plants have gone to seed.

A patch of Devil's-bit can be one of best ways of attracting nectaring insects to your meadow or garden. Isolated plants, or plants spread out in the meadow, are not as effective as a dense patch of plants, particularly growing in a sunny, sheltered position. From mid-August to early September even buddleia and marjoram take second place. One way of growing them in a garden setting is to plant seedlings through a mat into fertile soil. Without competition they will grow into enormous plants. The bigger the patch of Devil's-bit the better; it needs to be at least 2-3m^2 for the best results.

Field scabious likes free-draining soil with some fertility. Small scabious is one to grow in limestone chippings, or any area that is very poor and has some lime in the soil. You can break side shoots off a mature plant and grow them on. In the autumn, pull up the dead stalks of small scabious. At the base of the stalk there is usually a small piece of root. If you stick this in the ground it should flower towards the end of the following year. The knapweeds can be treated in the same way.

Sorrel. Small Coppers like to lay their eggs on young sorrel. The year after I had sown my meadow the numbers of Small Coppers increased; every year since then their numbers have declined. This may well be due to the turf getting thicker, leaving fewer areas of bare soil where sorrel can self-seed and male Small Coppers set up territories.

Sorrel seed germinates at a good rate and quickly. Sow in big seed trays in early April. Then, in late May or early June, plant it out into bare ground in mustard and cress-like clumps, ready for the second brood of Small Coppers.

Tansy. Tansy is another plant that provides nectar in late summer and, like fleabane, is a favourite of the Small Copper. Sow the seeds in a seed tray and leave out over winter. You only need to do this once, as it is a plant that spreads by underground runners. If you keep it in the border you can dig pieces up as you need them. It will compete with tall grasses so can be grown in the hedgebank.

Tansy, another favourite of the Small Copper.

Thistles. All the thistles are good nectar plants for butterflies and bees. In fertile soil, creeping thistle can spread rapidly, killing off areas of grassland as it grows above the sward and being more trouble than it is worth. In poorer soils, its ambitions are curtailed. But there are species of thistle far prettier than the creeping thistle: musk, meadow, marsh, spear and woolly. Musk and woolly are biennials, both plants worthy of growing in the border, where they will self-seed so you can transplant seedlings into the meadow. They are large plants and you only need a few. The musk thistle is a good butterfly plant; the woolly is more useful for bees.

The marsh thistle is another biennial, preferring a damp site, although it will grow in other areas. It is an important nectar plant in some butterfly meadows because it flowers in mid-June, before the knapweeds are out.

Meadow thistle is a perennial which likes the edges of marshy areas. It flowers before knapweed so is worth growing if you have a dampish bit of meadow where the grass stays reasonably short.

Marsh thistle.

In the garden the meadow thistle can grow quite tall.

Thyme.

Thyme. The aromatic foliage can be enjoyed by butterflies and non-buttterflies alike. Three species are commonly found growing wild. It's easy to grow from see on cuttings.

Tower Mustard. This biennual grows easily from seed sown directly on bare ground. Nevertheless, it is worth sowing some in pots each year to make sure that you don't lose it.

Tower mustard.

Valerian. Although not in quite the same league as marjoram and knapweed, in the right situation, valerian is still one of the best nectar plants. Ringlets crowd onto

Valerian.

large plants growing out of my hedgebank. It is one of the most versatile of wild flowers and can be grown almost anywhere. It increases by underground runners and, in a favoured place, may spread over quite a large area. Sow its seed in seed trays, cover with a sheet of glass and leave out over winter. You could also put a number of plants into the border, where it will spread readily and you will be able to dig up a few plants each year for planting out into the meadow.

Red valerian is a different plant altogether, commonly grown in gardens – especially on walls. It is an excellent nectar plant, best planted in an area of limestone chippings rather than the meadow.

Viper's bugloss.

Viper's bugloss. This is a stunning plant and one of the favourite nectar plants of the golden skippers, but it is a biennial and will only be persistent in a well-drained sandy or limey soil that has bare patches. It is still worth raising if you are creating a meadow, even for only one year of flowering. Sow it in seed trays and plant out the seedlings in the meadow when they are large enough.

Violets. The seed of violets is expensive but they can be propagated very easily by breaking off pieces of rootstock or runner from a plant growing in the border and rooting them in compost.

Hairy violet.

Hairy Violet is one of the best plants to grow in well-drained, limey grassland. You can make a hairy violet mound by heaping up topsoil to produce a mound with a flat top, laying a mat over the flat top and covering this with a thin layer of oolite or gravel. Break up a hairy violet plant into pieces, each with a little bit of root, and plant the pieces into the topsoil through slits in the mat. In the absence of competition, the violets will grow quite large and provide you with both plenty of new plants and a lot of seed. Uncollected seed will germinate in the gravel or oolite, providing you with yet another source of plants.

Other violets are more difficult to grow in open situations as they prefer cool, moist spots. Poor, sparse grassland is one place where they might survive; infertile soil underneath scrub that is cut back regularly could also work well. As soon as there is any competition they disappear.

Wild Privet. Wild privet is a good nectar source and grows easily from cuttings left in the ground over winter. Try putting the cuttings where you want the privet bushes to be, keeping the grass clear around them till they are well established. Alternatively, they can be bought from nurseries specialising in native British trees.

Wild Strawberry. This is the foodplant of the Grizzled Skipper. It spreads easily by runner in bare ground. Put some in your border and keep the ground cleared around it. Every year you will be able to remove new plants to put into your bank. Wild strawberry only does well in sparse grassland, or on areas of bare ground.

Wild strawberry.

Wych Elm. This is the food-plant of the White-letter Hairstreak. The caterpillar initially feeds on the flowers so it is important to plant trees which will flower well – not all do. Take softwood cuttings (in July) from trees that you have marked as flowering freely, or buy flowering elms from specialist nurseries. *Ulmas glabra* 'Camperdownii' is a weeping wych elm. Wych elm used to be less susceptible than common elm to Dutch elm disease but there are signs that this may be changing.

Wych elm.

Yellow Rattle. Yellow rattle is not of direct benefit to butter-flies – though I have seen Large Skippers nectaring on it – but it is still a useful species for the meadow-maker. As a semi-parasite on grasses it stunts the host by taking some of its nutrients. Other flower species then benefit from this reduction in vigour.

Yellow rattle is an annual and needs to set seed each year; if the meadow is mown early it will disappear. From late summer it can be sown directly into mown grass, or with a meadow mixture containing grass seed. Do not sow it in fertile areas as it is not robust enough to compete with the coarser grasses.

Yellow rattle.

Chapter Eleven
The Butterfly World

THE BUTTERFLY SEASON

The butterfly season can start early in the year, with Brimstone males patrolling the hedgerows, but it is not until late April or early May, if the weather is fine, that butterflies start to come out in reasonable numbers. In gardens you may see Small Tortoiseshells, Commas, Peacocks, Holly Blues, Brimstones, Orange-tips, Green-veined Whites, Small and Large Whites, and Speckled Woods.

In the meadow this can be a very exciting time, especially if you have created banks or

Brimstone nectaring on betony.

areas of low fertility. Butterflies will not be present in large numbers, though all the garden butterflies could be flying. But this is when a number of colonial butterflies emerge; the Common Blue and Small Copper, the Dingy and Grizzled Skippers, the Green Hairstreak, Brown Argus and Small Blue.

In June there is a brief lull as first brood butterflies die away, but by mid-June the Large Skipper heralds the explosive appearance of tho butterflies that lay their eggs on grasses. Golden skippers and browns abound (as well as some day-flying moths), and may well spill over into gardens close to their colonies. In the meadow, butterfly numbers will be at their peak by the end of July. In the garden, this is just the start of the build-up, with vanessids and whites dominating. Speckled Wood numbers will be at their highest and Brimstones make a comeback.

In the meadow, second brood Common Blues, Small Coppers and Brown Argus essentially bring the year to an end, though the Small Copper may be present deep into October if the weather is hot. After this, it is time to start tidying-up, strimming and cutting – and dreaming of the next butterfly season.

Recording Butterflies

It is interesting to take note of the butterflies that come into your garden. This is especially true if you are making changes to the garden with butterflies in mind. Keeping a record lets you see if your alterations have made any difference. The garden survey will also be welcomed by Butterfly Conservation (see below). If you have a large area of land it may be useful to create a transect.

The Transect

The succession of butterflies that comes to your meadow will be virtually the same each year, but the numbers of each species that emerge will be different. Without counting every butterfly in your meadow it may be difficult to tell how these populations are fluctuating. The butterfly transect is a way of counting butterflies that gives you an idea of their relative abundance: it can tell you, for instance, if there are more Meadow Browns than last year, or roughly the same as there were three years ago.

Record as follows: devise a walk that takes in most of the site and all the different habitats, then divide it into sections – as far as possible, one sort of habitat to a section. Experience of your own site is the best guide to these divisions, especially when it comes to deciding how long each section should be. In my own meadow, for instance, the section through the middle of the hay field, where fewer species fly, is 200m long; the bank with marjoram, the other hand, may have ten or more species flying at once, some in large numbers, and there it makes sense to keep the sections much shorter.

Each week, from April to the end of September, you walk the same route on your land and note the butterflies you see. You count only those butterflies within five metres of your route; you don't include those you can just see through binoculars at the other side of the meadow....

Each different species in each section is counted weekly, and at the end of the year the weekly counts of each species are totalled. Then you can compare with previous years the relative abundance of each species.

It is always fascinating to compare one season's figures with another. In the first years, numbers of butterflies in a newly-created habitat may be low because it takes a while for them to find the site, but keep a record from the beginning: it is important to know how the site is developing.

The transect results (and garden surveys) should be sent to the County Recorder at your

The transect walker.

local branch of Butterfly Conservation, who will also give you the survey forms you need and information about different ways of recording your data.

Transect walks are always carried out during the middle of the day, when it is warmest. In the evening it is interesting to observe another aspect of butterfly behavior: where they roost.

Butterfly Dreams

Towards the evening you will see many butterflies, with wings outspread, perching on grass stems. Their wings are orientated towards the sun, soaking up the last rays. Then slowly the butterflies disappear. Where do they go?

In my own meadow, the Brown Argus and Common Blues roost on long grass near the base of the bank; the Marbled Whites, Meadow Browns and some of the Gatekeepers and Ringlets roost on long grasses in the hay field. The Small and Essex Skippers also roost on long grasses, but while the Small can be found in a variety of places, the Essex chooses to roost at the lowest part of the hay meadow. On cool nights it can be difficult to find any of these species. Some may be in the trees surrounding the meadow. The Gatekeeper certainly roosts there.

Common Blue roosting in the long grass at the base of the bank.

Some butterflies and moths – for instance, skippers and the Marbled White – become so dopey when they roost that they can be gently picked up. Five- and Six-spot Burnets may be coaxed to crawl onto your hand for closer examination. Marsh Fritillaries are particularly quiescent. Butterflies like the Meadow Brown and Ringlet are more aware. If you do manage to coax one onto your hand, it will soon flutter off. Both these species will fly in coolish conditions during the day. It would seem that the butterflies that like warmer conditions are the ones made more comatose by the cool of the evening.

Photographs Today

As a child we used to go to the local museum to see the Egyptian mummies, the stuffed animals, and tray after tray of dead butterflies. I always found these exhibits depressing. Now people collect photographs of butterflies. One challenge is to photograph all the butterflies of the British Isles. With a good camera, the results can be wonderful, and it is a good excuse to visit beautiful and often dramatic landscapes. Even in the garden, if we look carefully, there will be sights to rival any in the Serengeti.

The Comma.

Breeding Butterflies

Some butterfly larvae may be reared in captivity. Small Tortoiseshell larvae, for instance, are easily found and are not difficult to rear in a breeding cage in your garden. Entomologists progress from breeding common butterflies to breeding more difficult species. In the Recommended Reading section, there are details of a number of publications that cover the techniques required to successfully breed British butterflies in captivity.

Breeding butterflies outdoors on their foodplant.

Chapter Twelve

Conserving Butterflies

Many colonial butterflies are on the northern edge of their European range in southern Britain. Here they are confined to warm spots, like south-facing hillsides. Many of these warm spots are isolated and this makes it difficult for individual butterflies to move from one spot to another, making such colonies vulnerable to extinction. Imagine a south-facing bank with a small colony of Dingy Skippers. Each May, a few adults emerge, but one year, after the first males have emerged, the weather deteriorates and for the next two weeks it is cool and rainy. The females emerge and sit in the long grass, getting wet. There is very little

Many rarer butterflies are confined to very warm spots in the south of Britain. The Adonis Blue is found on the warmest south-facing slopes of chalk and limestone downs. The grassland it likes is usually very short, some where horseshoe vetch grows in profusion. Further south in Europe, where the weather is generally warmer, it can be found in longer grassland and on north-facing slopes.

activity. The next year, only two or three adults emerge, and the following year, none. Nearby, on a larger site, there is a larger colony of Dingy Skippers. The same weather may cause the population to shrink but it is more likely that enough males and females will mate for the colony to persist. With a series of warm years this colony will increase in numbers and a few butterflies may stray onto the smaller site and re-colonise it. If that small site is too far away, however, the Dingy skipper would be lost to it for ever.

VULNERABLE BUTTERFLIES

Colonies on small, isolated sites, where visitors from other colonies are rare or non-existent, can also disappear because of inbreeding. They are also vulnerable to change in the management practise that has maintained that particular habitat.

Many of the important sites for butterflies are very small and there could well be colonies of butterflies near your house that you know nothing about: many areas are under-recorded. For instance, a walk you go on regularly could have a site that is home to a colony of Green Hairstreaks or Dingy Skippers. These butterflies fly for only a few weeks each year. During those weeks there will be a peak in the numbers emerging. If you walk by the site a couple of weeks either side of that peak you could be totally unaware of the colony's existence. Even if the time is right, unless the sun is shining the butterflies will be inactive, and again it would be easy to miss the colony. One approach is to look out for suitable habitats, generally warm, sheltered spots with sparse grass and lots of foodplants, then visit these sites during the period of peak emergence, choosing a time when the sun is shining.

It was observation of this sort that led Roger Sutton and Tony Leibert to discover what are today some of the best butterfly reserves in Somerset. After finding the first sites, they looked at local plant records compiled by botanists. When they located the plants, they found the butterflies. If you find such an area, you could record the species you see. It may even be a good place for a transect.

The wandering butterflies and some of the golden skippers and browns can utilize a lot of areas in the general countryside; the habitats that these butterflies like are still widespread. In fact, with global warming, some species are spreading to the north of their normal range. But even these butterflies are disappearing from areas within their range. Both the specialized butterflies and the more widespread species remain dependant on a network of colonies for their long-term survival.

Butterfly numbers and species have been declining over the last 200 years, but the 'improvements' in farming that took place after the Second World War escalated the decline. There are signs of hope – we now have a better knowledge of how to restore habitats – but it is the implementation of that knowledge we have to fight for. This is where gardens can help, by containing plants which support and add to scarce habitat for as wide a range of butterflies as possible .

CONSERVATION ACTIVITY

Any records of butterflies that you send to your local county recorder will be added to the Butterfly Monitoring Scheme for the United Kingdom (UKBMS), which is being co-ordinated by the Centre for Ecology and Hydrology, the Joint Nature Conservation Committee and Butterfly Conservation. In 2000, this information was used to produce *The Millennium Atlas of Butterflies in Britain and Ireland*.

Since then, along with the Dublin Naturalists' Field Club, the same groups have published *The State of Butterflies in Britain and Ireland*. Both books show the present distribution of butterflies in the two countries and are a guide to the butterflies found in your area. *The Millennium Atlas*

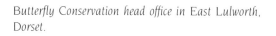

Butterfly Conservation head office in East Lulworth, Dorset.

also gives detailed accounts of the natural history of all these butterflies.

Records such as these are vital to understanding how best to conserve butterflies and, just as important, they provide biodiversity data. Because butterflies and moths are highly sensitive to changes in the environment they make valuable indicator species and have now been recognised as such by government agencies.

What can the individual do? Besides making a butterfly and moth garden you could join the campaigning organisation, Butterfly Conservation. Founded in 1968, the Society's main aim is to halt the decline of butterflies and moths. To this end, it advises landowners, conducts surveys, creates and manages nature reserves, lobbies government, works with other conservation bodies, does research, raises awareness of butterflies and moths, monitors butterfly numbers and encourages butterfly gardening. It produces a magazine three times a year, full of information about butterflies. Further information and contact details can be found on page 177.

Transect work for the society is always useful. Some of the most important transects are through farmland, where the walker can monitor the effects on butterfly numbers after the introduction of Countryside Stewardship schemes.

Of direct interest to the butterfly gardener, Butterfly Conservation has over 30 local branches. These provide an opportunity to meet others of a like mind, and exchange ideas and plants. Walks round prime butterfly habitats are led by butterfly experts. Many of the branches produce a transect booklet giving the results of all the transects walked in your county. Some also produce an annual atlas showing all the butterfly records for the year. This is very useful in determining how near colonies of butterflies may be to your meadow or garden.

THE FUTURE

With the advance of global warming, it becomes increasingly necessary for butterflies to have corridors of natural habitat through which they may move in order to extend their range. It is landscape-scale projects of this sort that will have the biggest effect on butterflies and butterfly movement.

Butterfly Conservation Project Officer giving advice to a landowner on Dartmoor.

Butterfly habitats can be made quite easily once the basic principles are understood. In addition to gardens, butterfly meadows could be made in parks, schools and other open public places. Farmers could create meadows on field edges. On roadside margins there would be no need to import expensive topsoil, and, with low fertility soils, management is simple since the area only has to be mown once a year. Even landfill sites can become covered in butterflies. Brownfield sites are sometimes the last refuges for those butterflies that are early successional specialists – those that like environments with little or sparse vegetation. When such sites are re-developed, this habitat could be duplicated on banks or even roofs.

We are never going to return to a time when continuity of management practises created an environment perfectly suited to butterflies. We can nevertheless reproduce – albeit on a small scale – wildlife habitats brimming with butterflies and moths. And if there are enough of these islands of habitat, butterflies will find them.

This is a site where one of Britain's rarest fritillaries, the High Brown, is found. Much work has been carried out by Butterfly Conservation on this hillside in Exmoor to help conserve this butterfly.

Sources

SOURCES OF MATERIALS AND INFORMATION

Substrates

Quarries are a convenient source of materials to use as substrates, although they are controversial for environmental reasons. There is quite a range of limestones, from soft rock, like chalk and oolite, to the harder, carboniferous limestones. Ground limestone is used extensively by farmers to 'sweeten' their fields, and limestone dust is used in the building trade for mixing with cement. There are also all the different sizes of chippings that the quarries produce. A telephone directory will list quarries in your area.

When roads or houses are built in an area of limestone or chalk, there are often large quantities of these substrates available, and the contractor may be keen to get rid of them. On a smaller sale, you could seek out waste products from monumental masons and other businesses that carve and shape limestone. Builders and masons are also worth contacting for their waste materials.

Seeds and Plants

If you hand-collect seeds you must get the landowner's permission. Do not collect seeds from an SSSI, or any other sensitive area. Only a very small proportion of most perennials' seed grows into an adult plant, so you will not be doing much harm to a wild site if you take a reasonable amount of seed; it is common sense not to collect all the seeds from all the plants, or take the seeds of rare plants. The plants that most butterflies depend on are relatively common.

The main problem with hand collection is knowing when seeds are ripe. If you collect seed throughout July and August and into the early part of September you should get a good range. Check the chart below to see which seeds germinate well when sown directly into the ground.

There are a large number of wildflower seed businesses, most of which have catalogues detailing seed mixtures as well as seeds of individual species. Make sure the seeds they sell are of British provenance.

Native plants and seeds

Emorsgate Seeds
Limes Farm
Tilney All Saints
Kings Lynn
Norfolk PE34 4RT
Tel. 01553 82902
www.wildseed.co.uk

Flowers Farms
Carvers Hill Farm
Shalbourne
Marlbourgh
Wiltshire SN8 3PS
Tel. 01672 870782
www.flowersfarms.com

Landlife
National Wildflower Centre
Court Hey Park
Liverpool L16 3NA
Tel. 0151 737 1819
www.landline.org.uk

For many more seed houses and nurseries see Flora Locale below.

Non-native plants and seeds
The Royal Horticultural Society
www.rhs.org.uk
The website will help you locate non-native plants.

Phoenix Perennial Plants
Paice Lane
Medstead
Alton
Hampshire GU34 5PR
Tel. 01420 650695

Large trees
If you want large trees to make an instant impact in your garden, consult
www.impactplants.co.uk

CD-Rom
Complete Gardens CD-ROM Ltd.
40 Davenant Road
Oxford OX2 8BY
Tel. 01865 512561
www.complete-gardens.co.uk
Good descriptions and illustrations of over 100 garden plants attractive to butterflies.

Organisations
Butterfly Conservation
Manor Yard
East Lulworth
Wareham
Dorset BH20 5QP
Tel. 0870 7744309
www.butterfly-conservation.org
The major organisation concerned with butterflies and moths in the UK. It offers practical advice on habitat management, and conducts surveys and monitoring. Details of how to participate and join are on the website.

Butterfly World Trust
www.butterfly-world.org
The trust set up to raise funds to construct Butterfly World, a major butterfly project planned for St Albans, Hertfordshire.

Carymoor Environmental Centre
www.carymoor.org.uk
This centre, built on a former landfill site, runs education programmes, particularly for schools. There is also a small wildflower nursery.

European Butterfly Conservation
www.bc-europe.org

Flora Locale
www.floralocale.org
Flora Locale is an initiative of Plantlife and the Institute of Ecology and Environmental management, coordinated by the Nature Conservation Bureau. Its main aims are to 'protect indigenous wild plants and plant communities from introduced species and varieties' by reducing the imported, non-indigenous varieties of British native (plant and seed) species. Flora Locale has produced a series of guidance notes which may be useful if you are thinking of sowing a meadow. Their website also has an extensive list of suppliers of British native plants and seeds.

Moths
www.ukmoths.org.uk

The Wildlife Trusts
www.wildlifetrusts.org
There are 46 Wildlife Trusts in the UK, as well as 52 Urban Wildlife Groups. Together they manage 2,300 nature reserves. The Wildlife Trusts' website has a list of all local Trusts.

Landlife
www.landlife.org.uk
For the last 15 years, Landlife has been sowing wildflowers in projects as diverse as derelict land restoration, road schemes, country parks and community woodlands. Most of the projects are in urban areas. The other half of Landlife is Landlife Wildflowers, which supplies wildflower seeds all over the UK, many of the seeds harvested from their own projects.

The National Wildflower Centre
www.nwc.org.uk
This centre at Knowsley, near Liverpool, was set up with the help of Landlife. Its main focus is the creation of new habitats. On site is a range of activities: wildflower gardening and conservation techniques, a research and development centre, a wildflower nursery, training in urban regeneration strategies, an environmental information exchange, and a visitor centre.

Meadow Flower Chart
The chart starting on the next page should be used as a guide, rather than as a prescription, as to where plants will, or will not, grow.

Meadow Flower Chart

	F	ST	M	pH	H	S	P	N	FP
Agrimony *Agrimonia eupatoria*	m, l	a, c, l	d, m	n, c		ss	✓		6
Alder Buckthorn *Frangula alnus*	H	l, c	m, w	a, n			✓		10
Autumn Hawkbit *Leontodon autumnalis*	m, l	s, l, c	d, m	a, n		✓		o	
Barren Strawberry *Potentilla sterilis*	H+g	l, c	d, m	a, n	v		✓		6
Betony *Stachys officinalis*	m, l	s, l, c, a	d, m	n, c		ss	✓	g	
Bird's-foot Trefoil *Lotus corniculatus*	m, l	all	d, m	a, n, c	n	✓		s	7, 9, 15, 22, 25, 44, 47
Bistort *Polygonum bistorta*	m	l, c	m, w	n	v		✓		
Bitter Vetch *Lathyrus montana*	m, l	l, c	d, m	a, n	v	✓	✓		8
Black Medick *Medicago lupulina*	m, l	s, l, c, a	d, m	n, c	n	✓			
Blackthorn *Prunus spinosa*	H	s, l, c, a	d, m	n, c	v		✓		16, 19
Bladder Campion *Silene vulgaris*	m, l	all	d, m	n, c		ss	✓	g	
Bloody Cranesbill* *Geranium sanguineum*	m, l	s, l, c, a	d, m	n, c	v		✓		
Bluebell *Hyacinthoides non-scripta*	H+g	l, c	d, m	a, n			b	o	
Bramble *Rubus fruticosus* agg	H+g	s ,l, c, a	d, m	a, n, c	v		✓	g	6, 15
Broom *Cytisus scoparius*	H+g	s, l, c	d, m	a, n	n		✓	o	
Buckthorn *Rhamnus catharticus*	H	s, l, a	d	n, c			s ✓		10

Buddleia *Buddleia davidii*	H+g	l, c, a	d	n, c			✓	s	
Bugle *Ajuga repans*	H+g	l, c, a	m–w	n, c	v		✓	g	
Bulbous Buttercup *Ranunculus bulbosus*	m, l	s, l, c, a	d, m	n, c		✓		o	
Burnet Saxifrage *Pimpinella saxifraga*	m, l	l, c, a	d	n, c		ss	✓		
Bush Vetch *Vicia sepium*	h, m	l, c, a	m	n, c		✓			
Candytuft* *Iberis amara*	l	su	d	c	a	✓		g	
Carline Thistle *Carlina vulgaris*	l	a, su	d	c	bi	✓		g	
Cat's Ear *Hypochoeris radicata*	m, l	s, l, c	d	a, n		✓		o	
Centaury *Centaurium erythraea*	l	all	d	n, c	a	✓			
Chicory *Cichorium intybus*	h, m, l	l, c, a	d, m	a, n, c		✓	✓		
Clary *Salvia verbeneca*	l	s, l, a	d	n, c	ss		✓		
Clustered Bellflower *Campanula glomerata*	l	a, su	d	c	ss		✓		
Cock's-foot *Dactylis glomerata*	h, m	s, l, c, a	d, m	a, n, c		✓			2, 4, 37, 38, 40, 42
Codlins and Cream *Epilobium hirsutum*	h, m	s, l, c	m, w	n, c	v		✓		
Comfrey *Symphytum officinale*	h, m	l, c	m, w	n			✓		
Common Bent *Agrostis capillaries*	m, l	s, l, c, a	d, m, w	a, n		✓			38, 39, 41
Common St. John's Wort *Hypericum perforatum*	m, l	l, c, a	d, m	n, c		✓			
Common Spotted Orchid *Dactylorhiza fuchsia*	m, l	l, c, a su	d, m	n, c		✓		o	
Common Storksbill *Erodium cicutarium*	l	s, l, c, a	d	n		✓			24

Common Vetch *Vicia sativa*	m, l	s, l, c, a	d, m	n, c	a	✓			
Corky-fruited Water-dropwort* *Oenanthe pimpinelloides*	m, l	l, c	m, w	n		✓		o	
Corn Marigold *Chrysanthemum segetum*	h, m	s, l, c	d, m	n	a	✓		o	
Cornflower *Centaurea cyanus*	h, m	s, l, c	d, m	n	a	✓		g	
Cowslip *Primula veris*	m, l	l, c, a	d, m	a, n, c		✓	✓		29
Crested Dog's-tail *Cynosurus cristatus*	h, m, l	s, l, c, a	d, m, w	a, n, c		✓			
Crosswort *Cruciata laevipes*	h, m	l, c	m	n	v		✓		
Crow Garlic *Allium vineale*	m, l	l, c	d, m	n, c		✓			
Creeping Cinquefoil *Potentilla reptans*	h, m, l	s, l, c, a	d, m	a, n, c	v		✓		6
Cut-leaved Cranesbill *Geranium dissectum*	h, m	all	m	n, c	a		✓		24
Dandelion *Taraxacum officinale*	h, m, l	s, l, c, a	m	a, n, c			✓	g	
Dark Mullein *Verbascum nigrum*	m	l, c, a	d	n, c			✓		
Devil's-bit Scabious *Succisa pratensis*	m, l	l, c, a	d, m, w	a, n, c		ss	✓	s	36
Dog Rose *Rosa canina*	H+g	s, l, c, a	d, m	a, n, c			✓		
Dog Violet *Viola canina*	H+g	s, l, c, a	d	a, n, c	v		✓		34, 35
Dropwort *Filipendula vulgaris*	l	s, l, a, su	d	c		ss	✓		
Dyer's Greenweed *Genista tinctoria*	m, l	l, c a	d, m	a, n, c		ss	✓		15
Evening Primrose *Oenothera biennis*	h, m, l	s, l, c, a	d, m	n, c	bi		✓	g	
Eyebright *Euphrasia officinalis*	l	all	d, m	a, n, c	a	ss			
Field Rose *Rosa arvensis*	H+g	s, l, c, a	d, m, w	n	c		✓		

Field Scabious *Knautia arvensis*	h, m, l	l, c, a	d	n, c		ss	✓	s	*36*
Figwort *Scrophularia nodosa*	h, m	s, l, c	m	n			✓		
Fleabane *Pulicaria dysenterica*	h, m	l, c	m	n	v	ss	✓	g	
Foxglove *Digitalis purpurea*	H+g	s, l	d, m	a, n	bi	✓			
Fragrant Evening Primrose *Oenothera stricta*	h, m, l	s, l, c, a	d	a, n, c	bi	ss		g	
Garlic Mustard *Alliaria petiolata*	h, m	l, c	d, m	n	bi	✓			12, 13
Germander Speedwell *Veronica chamaedrys*	m	s, l, c, a	d, m	n, a			✓		
Goat Willow *Salix caprea*	H	l, c	m, w	n	c		✓	o	
Gorse *Ulex europaeus*	H+g	s, l, c	d	a, n	n		✓	o	15, 22
Grass Vetchling *Lathyrus nissolia*	h, m	s, l, c	d, m	n	a	✓			
Greater Burnet *Sanguisorba officinalis*	m	l, c	m, w	n		ss	✓		
Greater Knapweed *Centauria scabiosa*	m, l	s, l, c	d, m	n, c		ss	✓	s	
Greater Stitchwort *Stellaria holostea*	H + g	l, c	d, m	n			✓		
Gromwell *Lithospermum officinale*	m, l	s, l	d	n, c			✓		
Hairy Violet *Viola hirta*	l	l, a, su	d	n, c			✓		35
Harebell *Campanula rotundifolia*	l	s, l, a, su	d	a, n, c		ss	✓		
Heath Spotted Orchid *Dactylorhiza maculata*	m-l	l, c	m	a, n			✓	o	
Hedge Bedstraw *Galium mollugo*	h, m	s, l, c, a	d, m	n	v		✓		
Hedge Mustard *Sisymbrium officinale*	h, m	l, c	d, m	n			✓		13
Hemp Agrimony *Eupatorium cannabinum*	m	l, c, a	m, w	n, c			✓	g	
Hoary Plantain *Plantago media*	m	l, a	d	n, c		✓			

Hoary Ragwort *Senecio* *erucifolius*	h, m, l	l, a	d	n, c		ss	✓		49
Holly *Ilex aquifolium*	H	l, c, a	d, m	a, n, c			✓		28
Honesty *Lunaria annua*	H	l, c, a	d, m	a, n	bi	✓			14
Honeysuckle *Lonicera* *periclymenum*	H	l , c	m	a, n	c		✓		30
Hop *Humulus lupulus*	H	l, c	m, w	n			✓		33
Hop Trefoil *Trifolium* *campestre*	m	s, l, a	d	n, c		✓			
Horseshoe Vetch *Hippocrepis* *comosa*	l	su	d	c		ss	✓	s	7, 26, 27
Kidney Vetch *Anthyllis* *vulneraria*	l	a, su	d	c		✓		g	21
Lady's Bedstraw *Galium verum*	m, l	s, l, al, su	d	a, n, c	v	✓			
Lady's Smock *Cardamine* *pratensis*	m	l, c	m, w	n		✓		g	13, 14
Large Bird's- foot Trefoil *Lotus* *pedunculatus*	h, m	l, c	m, w	n		✓		g	7, 8, 25 45
Lesser Calamint* *Calamintha* *nepeta*	l	a, su	d	c		✓		o	
Lesser Knapweed *Centaurea nigra*	h, m	s, l, c, a	d, m	n		✓		s	
Lesser Stitchwort *Stellaria* *graminea*	m	s, l, c	m	a, n			✓		
Marjoram *Origanum* *vulgare*	m, l	l, al, su	d	n, c		ss	✓	s	
Marsh Thistle *Cirsium palustre*	h, m	l, c, a	m, w	n, c	bi	✓		g	31
Marsh Woundwort *Stachys palustris*	h, m	s, l, c, al	m, w	a, n	v		✓		
Meadow Buttercup *Ranunculus acris*	h, m	s, l, c, a	d, m	a, n, c		✓		o	
Meadow Cranesbill *Geranium pratense*	h, m, l	l, c, a	d, m	n, c		✓	✓		

Meadow Rue *halictrum flavum*	h, m	l, c, a	m, w	n	v		✓		
Meadow Thistle *Cirsium dissectum*	l	l, c, a	m, w	n		ss	✓	g	
Meadowsweet *Filipendula ulmaria*	h, m	l, c, a	m, w	n, c		✓	✓		
Milkwort *Polygala vulgaris*	l	l, c, a	d, m	a, n			✓		
Mouse-ear Hawkweed *Hieracium pilosella*	l	s, a, su	d	a, n, c	v	ss ✓		o	
Mullein *Verbascum thaspus*	h, m	s, l, a	d	n	bi	ss	✓		
Musk Mallow *Malva moschata*	m, l	s, l, c, a	d	n, c		✓			
Musk Thistle *Carduus nutans*	h, m	a	d	c	bi	✓		g	31
Narrow-leaved Everlasting Pea *Lathyrus sylvestris*	H+g	l, a	d	n, c			✓	g	
Nettle *Urtica dioica*	H	l, c, .a	m	n	v		✓		32, 33
Nettle-leaved Bellflower *Campanula trachelium*	H+g	l, a, su	d, m	n, c		ss	✓		
Oak *Quercus spp.*	H	l, c	m	a,n			✓		17
Old Man's Beard *Clematis vitalba*	H	a	d	c			✓	g	
Orange Hawkbit *Hieracium brunneocroceum*	l	l, a, su	d, m	a, n	v		✓		
Orpine *Sedum telephium*	H	l, a	d, m	n			✓		
Ox-eye Daisy *Leucanthemum vulgare*	h, m, l	s, l, c, a	d, m	a, n		✓		o	
Pale St.John's Wort* *Hypericum montanum*	l	l, a	d	c			✓		
Pepper Saxifrage *Silaum silaus*	m	l, c, a	m, w	n		ss	✓		
Pignut *Conopodium majus*	m, l	l, c	m	n		ss			46
Poppy *Papaver rhoeas*	h, m	s, l, c, a	d, m	n	a	✓			
Primrose *Primula vulgaris*	H+g	l, c, a	m	n			✓	g	29

Privet *Ligustrum vulgare*	H	l, a	d	n, c	c		✓	g	
Purging Flax *Linium catharticum*	l	all	d	a, n, c	a	ss			
Purple Loosestrife *Lythrum salicaria*	h, m	l, c, a	w	n, c			✓	s	
Quaking Grass *Briza media*	m, l	all	d	n,c		✓			
Ragwort *Senecio jacobaea*	m, l	s, l, c, a	d	n, c	bi		✓	s	49
Raspberry *Rubus idaeus*	H	s, l, c	m	n	v		✓	g	
Red Campion *Silene dioica*	H+g	l, c, a	m	n		✓		o	
Red Fescue *Festuca rubra*	m,l	all	d, m	a, n, c		✓			39, 40
Red Clover *Trifolium pratense*	m, l	s, l, c, a	m	n, c	n		✓	o	25, 48
Red Valerian *Centranthus ruber*	l	su	d	n, c			✓	s	
Restharrow *Ononis repens*	l	s, l, a, su	d	c	n	ss	✓		25
Ribwort Plantain *Plantago lanceolata*	m	s, l, c, a	d, m	a, n, c			✓		
Rockrose *Helianthemum nummularium*	l	a, su	d	n, c			✓		15, 22, 23, 24
Rough Hawkbit *Leontondon hispidus*	m, l	s, l, c, a	m	n			✓	g	
Sainfoin *Onobrychis viciifolia*	m, l	a, su	d	c			✓		
Salad Burnet *Sanguisorba minor*	m, l	s, l, a, su	d, m	c			✓		
Saw-wort *Serratula tinctoria*	m, l	l, c, a	d, m	n		ss	✓	g	
Self-heal *Prunella vulgaris*	m, l	s, l, c, a	d, m	n, c	v	✓		o	
Sheep's Fescue *Festuca ovina*	m, l	s, l, a, su	d	a, n, c		✓			4, 40, 43
Sheep's-bit Scabious *Jasione montana*	l	s, l	d	a	a		✓	g	
Sheep's Sorrel *Rumex acetosella*	l	s	d	a	a	✓			20

Silver Birch *Betula pendula*	H	s, l, c, a	d, m	a, n			✓		
Slender St. John's Wort *Hypericum pulchrum*	l	s, l, c	d, m	a, n		ss	✓		
Small Scabious *Scabiosa columbaria*	l	a, su	d	c		ss	✓	s	36
Small Teasel *Dipsacus pilosus*	H+g	l, c, a	m	n	bi	ss	✓	g	
Smooth Meadow Grass *Poa pratensis*	h, m, l	s, l, c, a	d, m	a, n, c			✓		39, 41, 43
Sneezewort *Achillea ptarmica*	m	s, l, c	m, w	a, n	v		✓		
Sorrel *Rumex acetosa*	h, m	s, l, c, a	m	n			✓		20
Spiny Restharrow *Ononis spinosa*	m, l	l, c, a	d	n, c		ss	✓		25
Sweet Briar *Rosa rubiginosa*	H+g	l, a	d	c	c		✓		
Sweet Cicely *Myrrhis oderata*	h, m	l, c	m	n			✓		
Tansy *Tanacetum vulgare*	h, m	s, l, c, a	m	n	v		✓	g	
Teasel *Dipsacus fullonum*	h, m, l	s, l, c, a	m	n, c	bi	ss		g	
Timothy Grass *Phleum pratensis*	h, m, l	s, l, c, a	d, m	n			✓		2, 40
Toadflax *Linaria vulgaris*	m	s, l, c, a	d	n, c	v		✓		
Tor Grass *Brachypodium pinnatum*	h, m	a	d	n, c			✓		1, 2, 5, 40, 41
Tormentil *Potentilla erecta*	l	s, l	d, m	a, n			✓		6
Tufted Vetch *Vicia cracca*	h, m	l, c, a	d, m	n, c	n		✓		8
Valerian *Valeriana officinalis*	h, m, l	all	d, m, w	a, n, c	v	ss	✓	g	
Vervain *Verbena officinalis*	m, l	l, a	d	n, c		ss	✓		
Viper's Bugloss *Echium vulgare*	l	s, a, su	d	n, c	bi	ss		g	
Water Avens *Geum rivale*	m, l	l, c, a	m, w	a, n, c	c		✓		
Water Mint *Mentha aquatica*	m	s, l, c, a	w	n	v		✓	g	
Wayfaring Tree *Viburnum lantana*	H	l, a	d	n, c	l		✓		
White Campion *Silene alba*	m	l, c, a	d	n, c			✓		
Wild Basil *Clinopodium vulgare*	m, l	l, a, su	d	n, c	v	ss	✓		

Wild Carrot *Daucus carota*	m, l	s, l, a, su	d	n, c	bi	ss			
Wild Daffodil *Narcissus pseudonarcissus*	H+g	l, c	m	n			b		
Wild Strawberry *Fragaria vesca*	m, l	all	d	n, c	v		✓		6
Wild Thyme *Thymus praecox*	l	s, a, su	d	a, n, c	v		✓	g	22
Wood Anenome *Anemone nemorosa*	l	l, c, a	m	n, c	v		r		
Wood False Brome *Brachypodium sylvaticum*	H+g	l, c, a	m	a, n		✓			2, 37, 42
Woolly Thistle* *Cirsium eriophorum*	m, l	a	d	c	bi	ss	✓		
Woundwort *Stachys sylvatica*	H	l, c, a	m	n	v		✓		
Wych Elm *Ulmus glabra*	H	l, c, a	m	n			✓		18
Yarrow *Achillea millefolium*	h, m, l	s, l, c, a	d	n, c		✓		o	
Yellow Flag *Iris pseudacorus*	h, m	l, c, a	w	n, c		✓			
Yellow Rattle *Rhinanthus minor*	m, l	all	d, m	a, n, c	a	✓		o	
Yellow Meadow Vetchling *Lathyrus pratensis*	h, m	s, l, c, a	m	n, c	n		✓		8
Yorkshire Fog *Holcus lanatus*	h, m	s, l, c, a	d, m	a, n, c			✓		3, 37, 38

*Species with a restricted range

KEY

F–Fertility

H (hedge) Plants to form the hedge or grow under it.

H+g (hedge+grassland) Plants that normally grow in wood or hedgerow but in some situations also grow in grassland.

h (high) Plants to grow in the long grass.

m (medium) Plants to grow in the main meadow area.

l (low) Plants to grow in areas of low fertility. When choosing plants for substrates or mounds it is best to restrict yourself to those calcicoles that only grow in the medium to low fertility areas.

ST – Soil Type

s (sandy) Sandy soils are free draining and often infertile. Because nutrients are quickly leached out they have a tendency to be acidic. The range of plants that grow in them depends upon the organic content of the soil. Drought can be a problem and autumn sowing is recommended. If you sow without or with very little grass seed, be prepared to do some watering during the summer.

l (loamy) These soils are usually fertile. Best to strip the topsoil.

c (clay) Clay soils may be highly fertile and can be hard to make a seed bed in. Best to add a thin layer of some substrate, and sow into this.

a (alkaline) Although loamy, clay, wet and even sandy soils can all be alkaline, seed mixtures for meadows are often sold using this category. The meadows that we normally think of as alkaline are those on chalk or limestone slopes; the plants to sow to create this kind of grassland favour well-drained alkaline soils with low fertility.

su (substrates) Plants to grow on very poor areas, or mounds.

M – Moisture

d (dry) Plants that like dry or well drained soils.

m (moist) Plants that like moist soils.

w (wet) Plants that are adapted to soils with a high water table. These soils may be flooded during the winter.

pH

a Acidic soils.

n Neutral soils.

c Calcarious or alkaline soils.

H – Habit

a (annual) Plants like the cornflower and poppy provide colour in the first year of the meadow, then disappear. Others, like purging flax, yellow rattle and eyebright, will germinate again if they find gaps in the sward.

bi (biennial) These plants need to find gaps in the sward to germinate. May be grown elsewhere and seedlings transplanted.

c (cuttings) These plants can often be grown from cuttings planted in situ.

l (layering) Plants which can be propagated by burying part of a branch. Weigh down the section that is buried with a heavy stone.

n (nitrogen fixers) Plants that fix atmospheric nitrogen.

v (vegetative) Plants that spread vegetatively, usually by under- or overground runners. You only need to introduce a few individual plants.

S – Seed

✓ Some flowers perform well from seed sown directly into the soil in general meadow mixtures (80% grass seed, 20% flower seed).

ss (sparse sward) These flower seeds can be sown directly into the meadow; they do best with low soil fertility and little or no competition from grasses, during the first years of a meadow.

P – Plants

✓ Some plants have more chance of success if they are introduced as plugs or small plants.

b and r Bulbs and rhizomes

N –Nectar plants

o Occasionally visited by butterflies.

g Good nectar plants.

s Superb nectar plants.

FP – Foodplants

Numbers in italics indicate secondary foodplants. Some of the butterflies listed below are very rare.

Hesperiidae 1. Lulworth Skipper *Thymelicus acteon* 2. Essex Skipper *Thymelicus lineola* 3. Small Skipper *Thymelicus sylvestis* 4. Silver-spotted Skipper *Hesperia comma* 5. Large Skipper *Ochlodes sylvanus* 6. Grizzled Skipper *Pyrgus malvea* 7. Dingy Skipper *Erynnis tages*.

Pieridae 8. Wood White *Leptidea sinapis* 9. Clouded Yellow *Colias croceus* 10. Brimstone *Gonepteryx rhamni* 11. Large White *Pieris brassicae* 12. Small White *Pieris rapae* 13. Green-veined White *Pieris napi* 14. Orange-tip *Anthocharis cardamines*.

Lycaenidae 15. Green Hairstreak *Callophrys rubi* 16. Brown Hairstreak *Thecla betulae* 17. Purple Hairstreak *Neozephyrus quercus* 18. White-letter Hairstreak *Satyrium a w-album* 19. Black Hairstreak *Satyrium pruni* 20. Small Copper *Lycaena phlaeas* 21. Small Blue *Cupido minimus* 22. Silver-studded Blue *Plebius argus* 23. Northern Brown Argus *Plebius artaxerxes* 24. Brown Argus *Plebius agestis* 25. Common Blue *Polyommatus icarus* 26. Chalkhill Blue *Polyommatus coridon* 27. Adonis Blue *Polyommatus bellargus* 28. Holly Blue *Celastrina argiolus*.

Riodinidae 29. Duke of Burgundy *Hamearis lucina*.

Nymphalidae 30. White Admiral *Limenitis camilla* 31. Painted Lady *Vanessa cardui* 32. Small Tortoiseshell *Aglais urticae*; Red Admiral *Vanessa atalanta*; Peacock *Inachis io* 33. Comma *Polygonia c-album* 34. Small Pearl-bordered Fritillary *Boloria selene*; Pearl-bordered Fritillary *Boloria euphrosyn*; High Brown Fritillary *Argynnis adippe*; Silver-washed Fritillary *Argynnis paphia* 35. Dark Green Fritillary *Argynnis aglaja* 36. Marsh Fritillary *Euphydryas aurinia*.

Satyridae 37. Speckled Wood *Pararge aegeria* 38. Wall *Lasiommata megera* 39. Gatekeeper *Pyronia tithonus* 40. Marbled White *Melanargia galathea* 41. Meadow Brown *Maniola jurtina* 42. Ringlet *Aphantopus hyperantus* 43. Small Heath *Coenonympha pampilus*.

Day-flying moths 44. Six-spot Burnet *Zygaena filipendulae* 45. Five-spot Burnets *Zygaena trifolii* and *ssp. palustrella* 46. Chimney Sweeper *Odezia atrata* 47. Burnet Companion *Euclidia glyphica* 48. Mother Shipton *Callistege mi* 49. Cinnabar Moth *Tyria jacobaeae*.

PICTURE CREDITS

Michael Barry, 33L, 60L, 94M.
Butterfly Conservation, 165, 171, 172, 173.
Butterfly World Trust, front cover, 148, 136, 150-1.
Ken Dolbear MBE, back cover (Comma), half title page, title page, foreword, 16, 17, 19, 25R, 33T, 33M, 33B, 33FL,34, 36L, 37B, 41, 46, 49MR, 49B, 51T, 51B, 55, 60M, 60R, 61, 87, 94T, 94B, 96, 100, 119R, 136, 138, 139T, 139B, 140L, 153 Comma, 159 Cinnabar, 166, 167, 169.
Keith Gould, 27, 42R, 42FR, 95M.
Pat Jerrold ARPS, 45B, 49BR, 105, 126B, 139L.
National Museum of Wales, 42TR.
Edward Parker, 18, 52-53.
Basil Yates-Smith, 14-15
All other photographs and illustrations are by the author.

RECOMMENDED READING

Ash, H. J., Bennett, R. and Scott, R., Flowers in the Grass (English Nature, 1992).
Asher, J., Warren,M., Fox, R., Harding, P., Jeffcoate, G. and Jeffcoate, S., The Millenium Atlas of Butterflies in Britain and Ireland (Oxford University Press, 2001).
Chalmers-Hunt, J. M., Local Lists of Lepidoptera (Hedera Press, 1989).
Davis, A. and Davis, I., 'Managing Your Own Wildlife Site', British Wildlife, 9/6 (1998).
Dunbar, D., Saving Butterflies, A Practical Guide to the Conservation of Butterflies (British Butterfly Conservation, 1993).
Ekkehard, F., Breeding Butterflies and Moths (Harley Books).
Fitter, A., An Atlas of the Wild Flowers of Britain and Northern Europe (Collins, 1978).
Hammond, C. O., The Dragonflies of Great Britain and Ireland (Harley Books, 1983).
Hicken, N., The Butterflies of Ireland: a Field Guide (Rinehart, 1993).
Nature Conservancy Council, 'The Management of Chalk Grassland for Butterflies', Focus on Nature Conservation, No. 17 (NCC, 1986).
Leverton, R., Enjoying Moths (Poyser, 2002).
Lickorish, S., Luscombe, G. and Scott, R., Wildflowers Work (Landlife, 1994).
Lousley, J. E., Wild Flowers of Chalk and Limestone (Collins, 1950).
Mabey, R. and Events, T., The Flowering of Britain (Hutchinson, 1980).
New, T. R., Butterfly Conservation (Oxford University Press, 1997).
Parker D. M., Habitat Creation – A Critical Guide (English Nature, 1995).
Rothschild, M. and Farrell, C., The Butterfly Gardener (Michael Joseph/Rainbird, 1983).
Skinner, B., Colour Identification Guide to Moths of the British Isles (Viking, 1998).
Stevens, J., The National Trust Book of Wild Flower Gardening (Dorling Kindersley, 1987).
Stuart, D. D., Buddlejas (Timber Press, 2006).
Sutton R., 'Little Breach Butterfly Reserve 1974-1996', The Bulletin of the Amateur Entemologists' Society, 55/406 (1996).
Thomas, J. and Lewington, R., The Butterflies of Britain and Ireland (Dorling Kindersley, 1991).
Vickery, Dr. M., Gardening For Butterflies (British Butterfly Conservation, 1998).

County Publications. There are a number of books and pamphlets detailing the species to be found in each county. Some of the more recent ones are listed below. (For lists published in the previous two centuries, consult J. M. Chalmers-Hunt's book, Local Lists of Lepidoptera; see above.)

Berkshire
Asher, J., *The Butterflies of Berks, Bucks and Oxon* (Pisces Publications, 1994).
Baker, B. R., *The Butterflies and Moths of Berkshire* (Hedera Press, 1994).

Bedfordshire
Arnold, V., Baker, C., Manning, D. and Woiwood, I., *The Butterflies and Moths of Bedfordshire* (The Bedfordshire Natural History Society, 1997).

Cornwall and Scilly Isles
Frost, M. and Madge S., *The Butterflies of South East Cornwall* (Caradon Field and Natural History Club, 1991).
Penhallurick, R.D., *The Butterflies of Cornwall and Isles of Scilly* (Dyllansow Pengwella, 1996).
Smith, F., *The Moths and Butterflies of Cornwall and the Isles of Scilly* (Gem, 1997).

Dorset
Thomas, J. and Webb, N., *The Butterflies of Dorset* (Dorset Natural History and Archaelogical Society, 1984).
Thomas, J., Surry, R., Shreeves, B. and Steele, C., *New Atlas of Dorset Butterflies* (Dorset Natural History and Archaeological Society, 1998).

Essex
Emmett, A., Corke, D. and Pyman, G., *The Larger Moths and Butterflies of Essex* (Essex Field Club, 1985).
Corke, D., *Butterflies of Essex* (Lopina Books, 1998).

Fife
Smout, A. and Kinnear, P., *The Butterflies of Fife: a Provisional Atlas* (Fife Council, 1993).

Gwynedd
Whalley, P., *Butterflies of Gwynedd* (First Hydro, 1997).

Hampshire and Isle of Wight
Hampshire and Isle of Wight Butterfly and Moth Report. An annual report available from the Hampshire Branch of Butterfly Conservation.
Barker, A. and Budd, P., *The Butterflies of Southampton and Surrounding Area* (Hampshire Branch of Butterfly Conservation).

Hertfordshire
Sawford, B., *The Butterflies of Hertfordshire* (Castlemead, 1987).
Hertfordshire and Middlesex Butterfly and Moth Report. An annual report available from the Hertfordshire and Middlesex Branch of Butterfly Conservation.

Kent
Philp, E., *The Butterflies of Kent* (Kent Field Club, 1993).
Beavis, I., *The Butterflies of Tunbridge Wells and District* (Tunbridge Wells Museum and Art Gallery, 1996).

Lancashire
Hardy, P., *Butterflies of Greater Manchester* (PGL Enterprises, 1998).

RECOMMENDED READING

Leicestershire
Robertson, T., *Some Mid-Century Leicestershire Butterflies* (Leicestershire Entomological Society, 1994).
Russel, A., *Leicestershire Lepidoptera Recording Scheme: Annual Review* (Leicestershire Entomological Society, 1994 and 1995).

Lincolnshire
Duddington, J. and Johnson, R., *The Butterflies and Larger Moths of Lincolnshire and South Humberside* (Lincolnshire Naturalists' Union, 1983).

Northumberland
Dunn, T. C. and Parrack, J. D., *The Moths and Butterflies of Northumberland and Durham* (Northern Naturalists' Union, 1986).

Orkney
Lorimer, R. I., *The Lepidoptera of the Orkney Islands* (E.W. Cassey, 1983).

Scotland
Stewart, J., Barbour, D. and Moran, S., *Highland Butterflies: a Provisional Atlas* (HBRG, 1998).

Shropshire
Riley, A. M., *Butterflies and Moths of Shropshire* (Swan Hill Press, 1991).

Suffolk
Mendel, H., and Piotrowski, S. H. *Butterflies of Suffolk: an Atlas* (Suffolk Wildlife Trust, 1986).

Surrey
Collins, G. A., *Butterflies of Surrey* (Surrey Wildlife Trust, 1995).

Sussex.
Gay, J. & P., *Atlas of Sussex Butterflies* (Sussex Branch of Butterfly Conservation, 1996).
Pratt, C., A *History of the Butterflies and Moths of Sussex* (Sussex NHS, 1980).

Warwickshire
Smith, R. and Brown, D., *Lepidoptera in Warwickshire* 1900–1995 (Warwickshire Museum Service, 1998).

West Midland and Gloucestershire
Nicholls, A. and Williams, M., *West Midlands and Gloucester Butterfly and Moth Conservation Review* (3, The Deer Leap, Dalehouse Lane, Kenilworth, Warwickshire CV8 2HW).
Wiltshire
Fuller, M., *The Butterflies of Wiltshire* (Pisces Publication, 1995).

Yorkshire
Beaumont, H., *Butterflies and Moths of Yorkshire: a Millenium Review* (Yorkshire Naturalists' Union, 2002).

ACKNOWLEDGEMENTS

First of all, I must thank Clive Farrell for all his help, advice and encouragement. And, at Clive's Ryewater Nurseries, Leslie Pattenden, who was a mine of information when it came to cultivated plants. Also at Ryewater, thanks go to Ivan Hicks, designer of the Spiral and Prison gardens, and to Trevor Cuff, the man who 'moves the earth'.

Tony Liebert and I have walked down similar paths to create meadows for butterflies and his methods have added an extra dimension to the book. Jack Doyle, the first 'moundmaker' – thanks for the inspiration. Mike Bailey, my thanks for helping to guide me through the moth world.

Ken Dolbear's butterfly photographs were invaluable. Photographers – Dr. Michael Barry, Keith Gould, Pat Jerrold, Edward Parker and Basil Yates-Smith – I thank you. Butterfly Conservation, The Butterfly World Trust and the National Museum of Wales also provided photographs.

Special thanks must go to Miranda Spicer and Andrew and Susan Sutterby for all the hard work they have put into producing the book.

In various ways, many people and organisations helped in the book's making. Steve Bushell, Butterfly Conservation; Carymoor Environmental Centre; Coleford Wildlife Group; Dudley Cheesman, Marina Christopher, Kim Creswell, 'Mac' Edwards, Lyn Formison, Jack George, Rachel Hooton, Martin Lane-Fox, Dru and Minnie Montagu and all the committee members of the West of England branch of Butterfly Conservation: I thank you all.

My wife, Val, has helped through many different stages of the book, and my children, Alasdair and Ellen, have helped me not to become a butterfly bore.

www.alphabetandimage.com

Index